CAUTION: GOD AT WORK

ORBIS BOOKS
Maryknoll, New York 10545

Caution: God at Work

Paul G. Johnson

Library of Congress Cataloging in Publication Data

Johnson, Paul Gordon, 1931–
    Caution—God at work.

    Includes bibliographical references.
    1.   Providence and government of God. 2.   Theology.
I. Title.
BT96.2.J63   231'.5   75-7781
ISBN 0-88344-052-0

*To the few
who live on the hills above
and to the many
who live in the valleys below*

CONTENTS

Introduction

"Work out your salvation with fear and trembling, for God is at work within you, both to will and to work his good pleasure" (Phil. 2:12–13).

No human being knows what work is like for God. But the fact that God does work can be inferred from that record of his activity found in the Judeo-Christian Scripture, the record often referred to as the Word. The Word of God and the work of God provide mutual credibility for each other. To speak of God's Word without his work is to deprive faith of an empirical base, while to speak of his work without his Word is to rob faith of its frame of reference.

History is the drama of God's activity; the world is the stage it is enacted on. History-in-the-making can be related to God's activity just as were events recorded in antiquity. What the written Word does is to set forth the work of God in a particular time and place; it gives us a source and precedent for seeing that work happening in and around us today. The Bible is a window to the world through which we can look in and then look out.

Both the caution and the incentive to join God's Word and work in the world of today were derived from Paul's friendly counsel to the Philippians. One can hardly remain silent if the Almighty is providing motivation to proceed. At the same time, what an awesome thought to hold in mind.

Caution in exploring the work of God is necessary for much the same reason that warning signs are posted on roads and sidewalks where people are working. There are dangers to avoid. Open manholes can lie in the way of unwary travelers.

One of these pitfalls is ascribing to the activity of God whatever cannot be explained in some natural manner. An example of this is Archie Bunker telling his family that he had missed being struck by a heavy object because a "little voice" told him to get off his chair and reach for something on the table. Mike's question,

"How do you know the voice was God's,"—was valid, and his observation, "Maybe it was God who missed," more than humorous.

Another pitfall is declaring that the activity of God cannot be proved, that it is an assumption that can only be taken on faith. Too many philosophers and theologians, under the influence of Immanuel Kant and Sören Kierkegaard, have spoken about faith in such a way that intelligent persons have been led to conclude that God is a product of the imagination, brought to mind through faith alone. These men and women are unwilling to take the leap and they regard anyone who does as a fool. To them the place for "God" is in brackets.

The consequences of this "corrective" have been tragic for both laity and clergy, both professional and amateur theologian. The professional thinkers have been intimidated from identifying what God is doing in the world. Some theologians, reacting to overemphasis on future pie-in-the-sky, do write about the activity of God in the present, but they shy away from relating it to any specific current event or person. For example, Wolfhart Pannenberg maintains that God has a history with humanity and through humanity with his whole creation, but nowhere does he illustrate this thesis.

In *The Future of God* Carl Braaten excites the mind with the idea that "history is the means by which God reaches new decisions, makes up his mind, and alters the trend of things," but he leaves the reader hungry for one example. Dietrich Bonhoeffer teased the theological community with the notion that God is very much a party to what takes place in our time, but he did not say how or where, and he was executed by Hitler before he could do so. Peter Hodgson says that Jesus is present not everywhere in history but only in those words and acts which conform to the definitive word of faith, expressing it anew. However, he ends up trying to make a sale without showing the customer the product.

Ironically, the average person is bombarded every day with concrete examples of God acting in history; he reads about them every morning and hears about them every night. But he never realizes what he is reading and hearing because Walter Cronkite and his colleagues draw no relation between the events they describe and God. The impression conveyed daily is that news-worthy efforts are those of persons such as King and Kissinger, not Christ.

For the laity, the result is a Church and a world full of deists, people who believe in what God did, but are oblivious to what God does. This came through to me with startling abruptness when I was talking with two young members of my church who had been social activists during the turbulent sixties. "What does your God do?" I happened to ask them. Their faces took on a blank look and for a moment the question seemed to leave them both speech-less. Finally, the young man blurted out, "He doesn't do any-thing!" As the implications of this response registered, I found myself raising the question with other people just to see what they would say. To my amazement it seemed to stop conversation rather than start it, as if I had thrown some kind of curve ball.

The central theme of the Bible is that God is redemptively involved in the affairs of this world, especially as they relate to the pursuit of justice and peace, two prerequisites for his "kingdom." The lay mind, however, seldom gets beyond a belief in the exis-tence of God and the created order. (New born babes and bud-ding trees are enough to affirm that.) The persistent image is that of a deity who spent six days or so setting things up and then retired on the seventh to a state of heavenly rest, leaving the world to run on automatic pilot.

Most will agree that there is more to the Bible than page one. Those who read further, however, seldom associate the biblical theme with present events, partly because other questions are on their minds, and partly because the Bible appears to be about things that happened in the past. The main event was Jesus Christ coming to earth for a brief interlude of show and tell—1900 years ago. Consequently, those were "Jesus times." Ours today are not.

Of course, if that event was one in which God was involved, a perspective other than deism is needed. Even here, though, a biblical image gets in the way. When last seen Jesus was heading in the direction of "heaven," where God was believed to be, and, in spite of the honest efforts of Bishop Robinson to bring God down to earth, a deity up above is still a very comfortable one to have in mind, or out of mind.

I am not aware of any polls that have been taken on what people think God does, but implicit in the post-Vietnam conservatism that has flooded America is a hint of a probable majority response. A God who does nothing in the world today has a made-to-order image for those who prefer a similar relationship to the issues that challenge us.

This volume attempts to heal the rupture in the news, to bridge the void. One cue for it came from Pastor Johann Blumhardt, a late-nineteenth-century German, who made it a practice to read the newspaper from his pulpit in order to help his congregation keep up with God's rule in the world. Karl Barth used to say that a preacher should have the Bible in one hand and the newspaper in the other. For both men Scripture provided the perspective, but the events of the day provided the historical data.

This book also received impetus from many political and social events of the last fifteen years. These spoke to me. Policies and priorities to which God revealed a dedication in the Judeo-Christian Scripture have come alive, as if God were making me aware of them for the first time in my life. As an example, for me the word *détente* used to mean simply a relaxing of international tensions; now it moves back and forth from the front page of the daily newspaper to the heart of the New Testament, where breaking down walls of hostility is a special province of God. Joining the Superpower with the lesser superpowers, I could conclude that God did not die in Jesus or on the cover of *Time,* but "came to life" in him and has ever since been at work, through friend and foe alike, to reconcile the world to himself, and its inhabitants, therefore, to each other.

Another example: Discussing the activity of One who did not have to apply for a State Department visa to travel to Peking or Moscow aroused me to the need for caution, but finding a prudent path was easier with two American presidents preparing the way. The connection between the biblical message and the writings of Karl Marx is hardly a new discovery, but until the flights of Air Force One, it rarely found its way beyond the halls of academia. Even now one must expect some flak. Although most Americans are glad that the threat of holocaust has lessened, a level of suspicion and hostility lingers. The Pentagon still sees Red when it looks over the world situation; the working person, who has about three months' pay conscripted by the government each year to finance the fight against communism, does not find it easy to accept the thought that our enemies are now our friends. To go from the exchange of threats and insults to the exchange of ballet dancers and hockey teams has been confounding, especially when the latter appear before us live and in color on television.

The theme of this book is particularly appropriate in this area because a primary source of American suspicion of the Marxist ideology is its atheism. This causes us to think that communists do not believe in anything, that Marxism is either immoral or amoral and, therefore, cannot be trusted. This "theological issue" has, in part, motivated us for more than twenty-five years. It has been in the name of God, as well as country, that we have pursued our have-gun-will-travel reaction to what we assumed were the ideas of Marx. The conclusion to which this book leads, however, and toward which the chariot of history is racing, is that the people we have been seeking to kill or contain are as indebted to the Creator for their goals as we are for ours. The God who provided us with the rationalization to wage war can be seen as the reason to work for peace and for a global society of liberty and justice for all.

To the objection that I am artificially bringing God into these situations, I would respond by saying "only in a verbal manner." Biblical evidence indicates that God is already at work; the most I can do is point to God's presence. Cultural anthropologists may be right that some events and movements in history are the result of a dreamer's wish for an ideal in the midst of social upheaval. Such a dream can be hallucination during pain, starvation, or fatigue. Neither this nor a genetic explanation, however, can do justice to the inspiration experienced by Karl Marx or by Jesus Christ and the prophets. Moreover, there are no ultimate grounds for saying that such inspiration is entirely of human origin. There are grounds, though, for believing that God participates in it, as we shall discuss in Chapter 1.

A preliminary comment is in order regarding the statements for discussion that appear at the end of each chapter. Their intent is similar to that of Martin Luther when to initiate debate in 1517 he nailed ninety-five affirmative statements on faith and financial

issues to the church door at Wittenberg. The number of statements in this book is less, but the intent is to open up serious
discussion on issues attendant to the human-divine situation that
underlies the events of history reported in the daily news. The
purpose is similar to that expressed by Bonhoeffer in 1944 when
he noted that we must risk saying hazardous things if only to stir
up vital questions thereby. In literary terms, the purchase price of
a book is but a down payment. To truly own it, one must ponder it
out loud with other people.

I would like to express my appreciation here to Dr. Howard
Thurman for allowing me to use his poem on the last page. Dr.
Thurman, dean of Boston University's Marsh Chapel from 1953
to 1965, wrote this bit of free verse for his Christmas card in 1968.
Upon completion of the book the reader may find it singularly
appropriate.

CHAPTER 1

God's Published Word

In order to establish the basis for declaring that God is actively engaged in the pursuit of justice and peace, it is imperative to turn first to the text that makes such a claim possible, the Bible. Immediately, however, there is a problem.

It is fairly easy nowadays to illustrate the human side of the Bible. Thanks to scholars who have carefully studied its contents, we know that it contains some stories and ideas that reflect the thought patterns of the cultures it was written from.

But for this volume it is also necessary to accept the Bible as an authentic source of insight concerning my subject, as a work of God as well as of human beings. If it is *only* of people, if it reflects only human views, then it cannot say much about God's activity today, because it did not say anything about God's activity then. On the other hand, if it is of God, then it should contain clues as to his policies and priorities, which being his, will span the centuries and the generations.*

The evidence that the Bible is of God, as well as of man, will not satisfy everybody, but it will be sufficient for the open-minded, rational person, for the person who is willing to follow the lead of his or her assumptions back to their point of origin. Part of this evidence is the fact that in the Bible the existence of God is taken

---

*I am aware of the sexlessness of the Deity, the patriarchal culture of the Hebrews that gave rise to the exclusive use of the male pronoun, and to the male Jesus. I am also aware that "she" is no more sexless than "he," and that there is no neutral personal pronoun in English. While I have used "he" for both the Deity and a human being, I beg the reader to make any mental substitution he/she desires.

1

for granted—it is given—as it would be if God truly had a part in its inspiration. The biblical writers had no reason to question God's existence since they already had the answer in the confrontation or experience that motivated them to write. He had already demonstrated or proved his existence to their satisfaction.

Second, if the Bible is of God, one would expect it to be a book reflecting in part the times in which it was written, for a God who did not communicate in terms that people would understand could hardly have convinced anyone of his existence. That it contains man's words, as well as God's timely communication, is also a clue that God cares more about reaching people than about infallible utterances.

This leads to a third factor substantiating consideration of the Bible as the Word of God. When two persons are confronting each other, the only way in which they can truly get acquainted is to speak in some manner. The most frequent and universally experienced form in which such communication takes place is through language. Through words one person is treated to a visit inside the mind of another; hypnotism and truth serum are interested in the same thing.

What is true in interhuman relationships is also true in humans' relationships with God. Hypnotizing God is impossible, since he is not a physical object over whom one can cast a spell. Indeed, he is not an object at all, except when he so presented himself in Jesus. Human beings who are blessed with physical sight are at a total loss when it comes to seeing God. No one has seen God, and the Bible acknowledges this fact (see Isa. 64:4; John 1:18; 1 John 4:12; 1 Cor. 2:9–12). People have ears for hearing sounds, but there is no way that they can hear God unless he initiates some kind of communication. Human beings are so dependent upon his initiating some form of communication that they would not even know of his existence if he did not first make himself known to them.

The witness of the Bible is that God has taken this initiative, and it is on this premise that my case is based. Just as he verified his own existence, so too has he made known his own priorities. The Bible is the record of God's activity within a segment of humanity, but it is meant to inform the faith of all who are willing to explore it from that perspective. To receive its message, one must be open to the premise upon which it is founded: that God bears witness to himself.[1] It is not necessary to prove the existence of God; he has already done so in his own efforts to reach mankind.

The first event recorded in the Judeo-Christian Scripture through which God bears witness to his interest in the liberation of an oppressed people is the dramatic rescue of the Hebrew people from the clutches of the Egyptian pharaoh. It would seem that four hundred years of slavery would have blotted out their memory of God's promise to Abraham to make of them a nation; no doubt many had forgotten it. However, when God identified himself, through Moses, as "I Am," that was all he needed to say (Exod. 3:13–14). This Word revived their hope and quickened their spirit. For a people surrounded by polytheism and laboring (literally) under the impression that the one and only Creator had singled them out for a special assignment, this was weighty self-witness.

The reported drowning of the Egyptian army in the Red Sea points to God's use of force, but it must be seen against the violence done to the Hebrew people by the pharaohs for four centuries. Consideration must also be given to the fact that God first reasoned with pharaoh through Moses and Aaron to let the people go, and it was only after pharaoh broke his promise to do so for the tenth time that the incident described in Exodus occurred.[2] What really comes through there is not so much the exhaustion of divine patience as the revelation of God's dedication to the liberation of the oppressed.

SPEAKING THROUGH THE PROPHETS

God again bore witness to himself and his priorities after many generations had become history and the Hebrew people were securely established in the promised land. However, they had become a nation divided against itself, in more ways than one. Under the military leadership of Jeroboam II, the northern province had experienced unprecedented prosperity—that is, some of its people had experienced prosperity. Actually only a few had profited from the military victories of the king. And as the rich became richer and the poor became poorer, religion had degenerated to mere form and lip service (Amos 4:5; 5:21, 14).

Then, in the hills of the north, the shepherd Amos received a vision in which God revealed his disgust with the situation. So, Amos, unaccustomed to public speaking but armed with the Word of the Lord, left the familiar terrain of his four-legged sheep and trekked to the cities, where two-legged ones were lounging in the luxury of comfortable homes and summer houses, stuffing themselves with the meat of tender lambs and choice calves (Amos 6:4; 3:15). As one might expect, when he called the pampered women "cows of Bashan," he did not exactly generate their enthusiastic support. Nevertheless, with unwavering courage he told the affluent leadership: You "oppress the poor . . . crush the needy" (Amos 4:1). Descendents of the oppressed slaves in Egypt had become the oppressors, and God was not pleased with them.

Some generations later the same message was communicated in the southern province, where a similar condition had developed. Again, prosperity had come to the few on the wings of military success. In all this the leadership had defrauded the poor and filled their barns with grain extorted from the helpless peasants (Isa. 3:14). Property had been bought up so that the masses had no place to live (Isa. 5:8). Wealthy men's wives owned party clothes, negligees, and mirrors (Isa. 3:18–23), while the wives of the poor had little or no wardrobes and did not know what their own faces looked like. Israel and Judah had not yielded a crop of justice, but a harvest of poverty and misery.

One of God's messengers to the south was Isaiah, and, although he forecast a grim future, he held out a ray of hope. He, too, was treated to a vision, and in it he saw a time when justice would emerge, and out of justice would come peace. Swords would be beaten into plows for tilling the soil and spears would be made into hooks for pruning trees. Wars would, therefore, stop and military training would cease. In that day the battle gear and the blood-stained uniforms of soldiers would be used as fuel for fires (Isa. 2:4–5; 9:5). In Isaiah's vision, this time was linked with the birth of a child, a son who would also be called "Mighty God, . . . Prince of Peace." And because he saw this taking place on earth in the arena of human society, he noted, "and the government will be upon his shoulder" (Isa. 9:6–7). It was an economic-political burden that Isaiah saw this "man" carrying. However, the birth of this child would be unexpected, like a root rising out of dry ground, and upon growing up he would be rejected by his own people (Isa. 53:2–30).

Although Isaiah did not speculate on the time of the Messiah's arrival, he was quite certain that he would appear in God's name and do God's work; he would bring true justice and peace to all the nations of the earth.

Affirming this concern for the rights of all people were the statements of the Lord to Jeremiah, another prophet who emerged in the south:

Let not the wise man glory in his wisdom, let not the mighty man glory in his might, let not the rich man glory in his riches; but let him who glories glory in this, that he understands and knows me, that I am the Lord who practice steadfast love, justice, and righteousness in the earth; for in these things I delight, says the Lord (Jer. 9:23–24).

In addition to the explicit witness God made to himself through the prophets, there was an implicit one. There was a prophetic tradition among the Hebrew people, but there was no formal school to which men like those mentioned above could go to prepare for their mission. They had received no training in elocution, sociology, or theology. Like Jesus' disciples, they were unlettered men, yet they were articulate and bold. For the most part they were men from the country, unaccustomed not only to public speaking but also to rubbing shoulders with politicians and kings; yet, they spoke the truth unflinchingly. Where did their knowledge come from? There was no visible source for such inspiration. There is no human way to understand how such verbal fires could be lit in the minds of such men. Their sensitivity to the plight of the poor can be understood, assuming they had opportunity to observe the luxuries of the rich. But admitting such an exposure, such a sensitivity, however, does not say how they found words, how their silence in the face of suffering could suddenly give way to the spoken truth. That such verbalizing would be attributed to the Unseen God is obvious, and perhaps intentionally so. What better way to bear witness to yourself and to your priorities than to have a person speak whose very occupation would call for a power greater than himself to help him?[3]

SPEAKING THROUGH THE SON

Several centuries later, a man who looked and talked like the original hippie stalked into the region around the Jordan River, calling for valleys of poverty to be filled with mountains of wealth—the very thing Isaiah had said the Lord would bring about upon his arrival (see Luke 3:4–6; Isa. 40:3–5). When John likened the "haves" to a brood of snakes, they became a trifle upset; some even asked him what they should do. "He who has two coats," he replied, "let him share with him who has none; and he who has food, let him do likewise" (Luke 3:10–11). But this was not all John the Baptist did to "prepare the way of the Lord." He also employed a rather extreme contrast in order to direct attention to Another. He said the One whose arrival he was announcing was so great in comparison to himself that he would be unworthy even to carry his sandals (Matt. 3:3, 11).

The union of the Mighty God, Prince of Peace, and the Son took place nearly two thousand years ago. In the life, death, and resurrection of Jesus Christ we see God's identification with what he said and did. This identification first came through his birth. He was born of a peasant girl, rather than a queen, prompting her to say that God had bypassed the proud and bestowed honor on one of low degree (Luke 1:46–52). Both the tribute and the reality bore witness to the God who had made his priorities known through the prophets.

Shortly after Jesus' birth, king Herod unwittingly revealed that this newborn son was the heir-apparent to the throne of the world by seeking to destroy him. The news of the Bethlehem birth so filled Herod with fear that, just to be on the safe side, he had all the male infants in the town slain (Matt. 2:16). That a king would find Jesus a threat to his power and position historically underscores the promise of Isaiah that upon this child's shoulders would rest the world's policies and political destiny.

When Jesus was a mature man, his words and deeds revealed

that he had come not to cancel the laws of Moses or to obliterate the prophets' vision of social justice but to fulfill them, to make them come true (Matt. 5:17). So tenacious was his belief in God's kingdom of justice and peace that he quoted Isaiah to the people of his hometown, "The Spirit of the Lord is upon me because he has annointed me to preach good news to the poor. He has sent me to set at liberty those who are oppressed" (Luke 4:18; Isa. 61:1–2). Economically, his audience was ripe for his news. Theologically and psychologically, however, there was a problem. Although a belief in life after death is not prominent in the Judaic Scripture, during the period between the Old and New Testaments, it took on inordinate importance. The thought of paradise emerged as a surrogate for what could not be achieved here on earth, and the outward observance of many ceremonial laws was extolled by the Pharisee party as the way to get there (Matt. 23:1–4). In the presence of these religious folk, the less-privileged masses felt like outsiders. As with the untouchables in relation to the Brahmin caste of India, the Hebrew masses felt more like sinners than saints; the law and the future weighed heavily upon them (Matt. 9:10–13).

The task that confronted Jesus, therefore, was to break the life-hereafter spell that religion had cast and to open up new possibilities for living together now. An example of the latter was his exhortation to love one's enemies, a way of implementing the prophetic desire for justice and peace. Jesus focused his attack primarily on the Pharisee's way of "getting to heaven"—the external observance of laws. By applying the penalty for killing to the angry impulse that fathered the deed, Jesus made the surface route impossible to travel. At times he spoke with devastating irony. "Unless your righteousness exceeds that of the scribes and Pharisees, you will never enter the kingdom of heaven," he informed people (Matt. 5:20).[4] To some this was like being told that the clergy didn't have a chance, and if they didn't who did? But such a statement turned attention to what truly did matter in this world, the point penetrated, and people observed that this was the truest word they could recall hearing from a man of God in a long time (Matt. 7:28–29).

Although the ethical principles enunciated in the Sermon on

the Mount were unprecedented, Jesus did not speak of them as
an ideal for some future kingdom. Rather did he speak of them to
motivate living as if that kingdom were already here. Indeed,
when Jesus did refer to a "kingdom of heaven," he seldom described an ethereal habitat in the sky, but rather earthly situations
and human experiences, such as a banquet, a setting whose dominant feature is food for the stomach. First on the revised guest
list were the poor, people with a gut appreciation for the menu
(see Luke 14:15–25). Some students, of course, claim that here
Jesus did not mean the poor in a literal or economic sense, but
they are hard pressed not only to say who the guests are in this
life, but also to explain what Jesus meant when he said the same
thing—in a literal not a figurative sense—to his host at a dinner
party. He suggested to him that next time he invite the poor,
rather than friends, relatives, and affluent neighbors who would
pay him back with ease (Luke 14:12–13).

To be sure there were occasions when Jesus sought to communicate a spiritual meaning. He did say, "Blessed are the poor in
spirit, for theirs is the kingdom of heaven." On the other hand, he
also said in the very next breath, "Blessed are the meek, for they
shall inherit the earth" (Matt. 5:3, 5). And if we move from
Matthew's account of this Sermon on the Mount to its counterpart
in Luke, the Sermon on the Plain, any inclination to spiritualize
the economic level of Jesus' teaching is completely ruled out (see
Luke 6:20–25). One interpretation is that "heaven" is made the
lure for leveling inequities on earth. Another is that it all occurs
on earth. Either way, Jesus promised to rich and poor alike that
one day the tables would be turned. Either way, Jesus revealed a
deep dissatisfaction with the rich-poor split in Palestin-
ian society.

If it wasn't for a long-practiced inability to hear what Jesus was
really saying, no affluent person today could read or hear these
words and not be deeply disturbed about his style of life. One
wonders what impact they made on those who first heard him
speak.

To be sure, Jesus was concerned about man's relationship to
God, but even when he revealed the redemptive nature of God's
good will, he usually made a social context the vehicle for his

teaching. Take, for example, the parable of the man who hired the unemployed at the end of the day and then paid them the same wage as those who had worked a full shift (Matt. 20:1–16). The paramount content Christ wanted to teach through this story was the impartiality of God's grace. However, to speak of this content only, ignoring the social implications that permeated his use of such a situation, is to do his compassion an injustice.

The God we see at work in Jesus Christ is no longer confined to a sacred location beneath the holy city's great dome. The human being is his temple and the streets his territory. He is no longer locked into the mental constructs of the chief priests. There were occasions when Jesus issued the threat of eternal punishment —especially for the rich and the powerful (see Mark 9:42–48). There were also times when he promised a heavenly reward for service rendered (Luke 14:14). Perhaps he did the latter to establish contact with people who were anguished by these ideas. But even when he employed such language the service he endeavored to inspire was for the benefit of others.[5] We see, therefore, that Jesus' primary message was love for the sake of the recipient, the kind of love God gave to man, the kind demonstrated through his own life style, through his own death, and, three days later, through God's Easter seal of approval.

Amos and Isaiah, Jeremiah and Jesus lived many centuries apart and in different societies. Yet they shared a concern for justice and peace. Why? Though each was rejected by persons in positions of power and affluence, each believed God was his source of support and inspiration. Why? To say they compared notes is not enough, for Isaiah and Amos were long gone by the time Jeremiah arrived on the scene, and the latter joined his predecessors 400 years before Jesus was born. Perhaps the answer is in the first why. If over a period of one thousand years the leading voices for justice and peace were moved, in the face of opposition, to identify such concerns with God, it would seem reasonable to conclude that the God of the Bible was revealing his commitment to such goals and purposes through them.

ISSUES FOR DISCUSSION

1. God cares more about communicating with people than about making infallible utterances.

2. To understand the biblical message one must be willing to accept its premise: God bears witness to himself.

3. The underlying message of the prophets is that God is dedicated to lifting up the poor.

4. The drowning of pharaoh's troops was a minor violence compared to the Egyptians' treatment of the Hebrew people for centuries.

5. That unlettered, inarticulate shepherds could suddenly find words for their feelings is a witness to God's activity.

6. The birth of Jesus is in harmony with the priorities God reveals through the prophets.

7. When it comes to economic concerns, we have a long practiced tendency not to hear what Jesus is saying.

8. When we take seriously what Jesus said about liberation and justice, he takes on the character of a revolutionary.

NOTES

1. This is true of any book. In order to get the message, the reader must be willing to begin where the author either implicitly or explicitly begins.

2. God's hardening of pharaoh's heart is a problem, but see Exod. 5:1; 7:16; 8:1; 9:1; 10:3.

3. Paul reflects a consciousness of this as it relates to his own link with God. See 1 Cor. 2:3–5; 2 Cor. 12:9.

4. One also thinks of the statement about it being easier for a camel to go through a needle's eye than for a rich man to enter heaven (Matt. 19:24).

5. For example, in the case of the party-giver, the benefactors would be the poor, the crippled, the lame, and the blind.

CHAPTER 2

Heaven—The Place to Go

How is it that one who spent well over twenty years in a carpentry shop, making chairs, tables, and beds, has become associated with a religion that for many has "no connection with life"? How is it possible that one who revealed a deep and abiding concern for the economic plight of the masses can be thought of as dwelling in a city with gold-paved streets? Why is it that one who walked and talked on earth, who demonstrated a concern for feeding the hungry and healing the sick is now considered by many to be seated on a distant throne, the monarch of a realm where there is neither hunger nor disease? The historical development of this dichotomy, plus some modern overtones, is the subject of this chapter.

The witness God made to himself in the life, death, and resurrection of Jesus drew about itself a group of followers, and—for a while—the spirit and direction of his charisma continued through that inner circle known as the apostles.

In Jerusalem, under the leadership of Simon Peter, both the social and personal dimensions of the gospel were evident.[1] At a gathering held late in the afternoon, "haves" and "have nots" sat at the same table, with food and drink provided by the more prosperous; at the close of this meal the Eucharist was celebrated. The two experiences *together* were called the Lord's Supper. The reflective nature of the second phase encouraged people to thank God individually for the friendship shared in the first.

In this climate the gospel had power, so much so that it moved those in and around Jerusalem who came under its influence to sell excess real estate and turn the proceeds over to the apostles for distribution to those in need.² Poverty disappeared from the group. When thought was given to the implementation and application of the gospel, this effect was bound to follow. The gospel inspiration was so strong that when two of these very early Christians, a couple named Ananias and Sapphira, sold some land and then held back part of the receipts under the guise that they had given the whole amount, death came to them (Acts 5:1–10). Thus, we see that Karl Marx was not the first to set forth the value of communism, nor were his Russian, Chinese, or Vietnamese sympathizers the first to employ harsh measures in implementing its ideal.

But elsewhere the infant church began to feel growing pains. Writing to Jewish Christians outside Palestine, James had to chide them for showing preference to the rich over the poor—and in church, of all places.³ Members were making a lot of fuss over visitors dressed in expensive clothes, giving them the best seats while others more shabbily dressed had to stand. What John wrote applies here, too: It is unthinkable that someone could love the unseen God and detest a brother in plain view (see 1 John 4:20). That John and James had to put such thoughts into words suggests that the readers of their letters were finding it possible to respond to God's love in Jesus without sharing that love with some of their fellow citizens.

What was beginning to surface was a split between faith and love. This dichotomy showed up most in the writings of Paul. At times he seemed to make the love relationship among people more important; at others, the faith relationship of man to God took precedence. It was Paul who said that of faith, hope, and love, the greatest is love. However, it was this same gentleman who said that the just shall live by faith. The two—faith and love—are inseparable, but in his letters Paul emphasizes one thing to the people in Corinth, and another to those in Galatia, Ephesus, and Rome.⁴

Presumably Paul had introduced the Lord's Supper of Jerusalem to Corinth, but, in his absence, both faith and love suffered. The persons who brought the food did not share it with those who had none, even though this meal was in the Lord's name, until Paul wrote to tell them that they were only kidding themselves. (Perhaps at this point Paul would have agreed with James that faith divorced from love was dead). He had to advise them to eat the main meal at home, and to share only bread and wine when they assembled, so the Lord's Supper would, at least, retain a spiritual dimension (1 Cor. 11:17–34). Unfortunately, the social dimension was hereby lost, and to this day his advice seems to have prevailed when it comes to celebrating the Sacrament; church suppers there are, but never in conjunction with Holy Communion.

In seeking an explanation for the development of this split, the sociologist of religion would quickly say that it happens in every movement as followers get further and further removed in time from the charisma of the founder.[5] However, with Christianity there is more involved, and it is helpful in understanding our own times and God's activity to take this briefly into account.

THE UNANNOUNCED GOAL

In retrospect, one can spot a tip-off that trouble lay ahead in the account of Christ's visible departure forty days after Easter, when, according to Luke, he ascended into heaven. So captivated were the disciples with the lift off and destination that it was necessary to say to them, "Men of Galilee, why do you stand looking into heaven? This Jesus . . . will come in the same way as you saw him go into heaven."[6]

This was one occasion when out of sight did not end up out of mind. Later in the first century, when Nero ventilated his fiery fanaticism on the Christians, the memory of where Christ had gone was a great source of comfort. When his followers awaited execution in the dungeons of Rome, the vivid descriptions provided in the book of Revelation were desperately needed and yearningly received.[7]

In Jerusalem, the ascension and the words directed to the disciples had produced a different effect. One reason communism died there in the first century was that the return of Jesus was thought to be imminent, so provision for the distant future was considered unnecessary.[8] However, when the money received from the sale of excess property gave out and the kingdom did not emerge, poverty reappeared.

As the years became decades and the Lord did not visibly return as promised, Christians had to rethink this aspect of their faith. Christians in Jerusalem had to settle for their pie in the sky rather than here on earth. In Rome, Paul, for one, revealed a change in view as he adjusted to the likelihood that he would die before the Day of the Lord.[9]

With the thought of Jesus' return pretty much up in the air (pun intended), revising the time of arrival was both necessary and possible. But in doing so the location of Christ became fixed in first-century thought: It was the direction Jesus had gone in taking leave of earth. The Christian concept became one of the Spirit being present on earth, as promised, and both God and Jesus being in heaven above. To this day the effects of this idea linger.[10] For a space-conscious age it suggests that God *qua* God does nothing. For many a lay person it shows up in the observation, "We're all going to the same place." For Bishop Robinson this led to his writing a best seller in the first half of the 1960s. And, as the Bishop observed, the notion of Christ coming to earth like a visitor from outer space—and then returning there—underlies every popular presentation of the Christian drama of salvation.[11]

This notion also made heaven the goal of Christians throughout the centuries, consciously sought, or unconsciously motivating activity and thought. Since this provides the backdrop for much in the Bible itself, the separation of faith and love was assured. Some of the dynamics deserve attention. For example, with heaven thought of as home, getting there assumed extraordinary importance. Because reaching it seemed a long way off, many persons focused concern on what to do in the meantime. Trusting in Jesus for salvation somehow did not seem to be enough. What to do here on earth was spelled out clearly in the prophets and in various teachings of Jesus, but with eyes now trained on the pearly gates, such priorities were sidetracked.

Unless there were powerful, soul-stirring preachers to remind people of the graciousness of God, it became hard to maintain a "religious feeling" (the perennial surrogate for thinking it through). In Galatia and Ephesus Paul discovered that people had gravitated toward other ways of achieving a religious image, such as regulations on eating and the observance of certain days and months as more holy than others (Gal. 4:8–11; Col. 2:16–19). It was as if in the failure of Christ to return on schedule and of God to have kept this phase of the promise, the announced plan had fallen apart, and now it was every man for himself. The result was that God's good will in Christ ceased to be the focal point of faith, and a new faith (an old one really) appeared: faith in one's own works. Human effort became the way of salvation. Concern for the needs of others, which God's love in Jesus had inspired at first, was replaced by a preoccupation with heaven and by the need to individually fulfill various religious rules in order to get there.

Paul tried to offset this do-it-yourself salvation by writing that the efforts of man to obey God's laws had proved futile, suggesting, though he did not say it, that the tendency to substitute man-made rules for God's desire for justice and love was proof of this failure, both for Jews and Christians. Since such failure indicated just how much man needs God's forgiveness, Paul went one step further. He concluded that the law of Moses had been given especially to make people realize this need (Gal. 3:23–24). Although this conclusion did not cancel the law in theory, it did in practice, causing many to assume that the teachings of Jesus concerning human relationships were so far beyond human capacity that the only recourse left was to plant one's faith in the redemption seen on the cross. After all, had not Paul himself written that he desired to know nothing among his people except Jesus Christ and him crucified (1 Cor. 2:2).

UP AND DOWN THE STAIRS

In keeping with the concern for heaven that appeared in the first centuries, two motifs shaped the history that followed them, both of which have left their mark upon us to this day. Each was related to the other and both contributed to the emphasis on faith gaining further preeminence over emphasis on love and/or justice.[12]

One was a preoccupation with doctrine and correct belief. This came in response to the presumed threat of certain movements such as Gnosticism (Jesus was the last in a long line of celestial personages sent to inform a select group of persons on earth that they were divine), Marcionism (the Old Testament and its God are to be rejected by Christians), and Arianism (Jesus was neither fully God nor fully man, but in between), to name a few. Since the climate was not so pluralistic as the 1970s in America Church-wide councils were convened to settle who was right and who was wrong in these doctrinal disputes. From these the Nicene and Athanasian creeds emerged, which are with us today.

The other motif, inseparably related to the first, was that of the power and organization of the Church. To safeguard the Church from the above threat, it was deemed necessary as early as the third century to set apart leaders who on a full-time basis could define what Christians believed. Hadn't Jesus said, "The blind cannot lead the blind" (Luke 6:39)? If others were to comprehend the faith, the leaders certainly had to. In achieving this end, however, financial support of leaders who had families of their own was undertaken by the congregations. Slowly, perhaps imperceptibly, a split between laity and clergy developed, together with the divorce of faith from love, and heaven from earth. From that time on, as historian Edward Gibbon observed, leaders in the Church spent more time exploring the nature of its Founder than in implementing his teachings.[13]

Paul had at least held the redemptive tension between faith and love firmly in his own mind. But in the Church from the third century on a professional clergy focused attention on man's faith relationship to God, at the expense of man's relationship to man. What subsequently became known as Christianity in the Middle Ages was an imperial state church, ecclesiastical structures, institutional schisms, and power struggles. From this milieu the crusades took their roots. Whether the issues were settled with pen or sword, however, during these centuries it was done in the name of faith, not love, for as Luther said, in reflecting on his own time, "Love does not curse or take vengeance, but faith does."[14]

There were exceptions, such as Francis of Assisi. Aiding peasants in the fields and caring for lepers became his priority in life and his understanding of Jesus. Some mendicant orders called for vows of chastity, poverty, and obedience, and no doubt there were many unsung heroes of the faith—bishops, priests, and laity—who sought to live out the love that Christ had for people. The demarcation of laity and clergy, however, produced a double standard in the Church: alms (gifts) for the poor were given by the rich but those who collected them were called religious. A member of the faithful or the religious was assured an ecclesiastical passport to heaven by doing what was expected of him, each in his own realm. Even generosity was conditioned by the prospects of one's future with God.

As decades became centuries, the seeds of distortion grew. By the sixteenth century clergymen had come to believe it was their prerogative to sell pieces of paper that assured the buyer he had purchased God's reprieve. The vertical direction which man had to take to reach God was symbolized by the holy steps in Rome, where the faithful could take years off time in purgatory by saying so many Our Fathers on each step. The priest was now the full-fledged mediator between man and God; inside the church his service was performed at the altar.

Because the Church now taught that the relationship between man and God required a go-between, the issue with which Martin Luther was really struggling was God's attitude toward failure to do his will, in other words, the nature of the Deity. When he discovered in Scripture, upon which centuries of dust had gathered, that God is merciful, that salvation is a gift, not a commodity, it was as if the door to heaven itself had been thrown open.[15] The grace of God makes faith redemptive, as the early Church had seen. Faith in Christ, not in the veneration of relics or in acts of contrition, was the New Testament way of salvation, and the only way to actually see this grace was to focus on grace alone. Luther's insight was that it is not necessary for man to climb up to God because he had descended those steps in Christ, greeting humanity on the first rung, the ground floor.

To keep the graciousness of God in sight, Luther maintained a distinction between the gospel—what man could believe concerning divine forgiveness—and the law—what man must do in relation to his fellow men. He saw the doing of good works for the purpose of chalking up brownie points with a heavenly father as contrary to the good news, but he did not for one minute say good works are unnecessary. He taught that they are not necessary for "getting to heaven," but for living on earth they are imperative. In matters of faith and conscience what counts is the gospel, but in everyday relationships what matters is "Moses and the law books."[16] Had Luther included "the prophets," he would have been closer to resolving the tension with which Paul had struggled, and might have spared many of his followers suffering and death, as we shall see.

Although Luther saw God's compassion as the key to the eternal kingdom, it would be wrong to convey the impression that he rejected the prevailing notion of God's wrath. What he did was to shift the implementation of God's wrath from the Church to the state, and for many in the German population this spelled subsequent disaster, both in the sixteenth century and in the first half of the twentieth. (Indeed, the issue involved here is one with which our own country is wrestling at the present time, but this will be discussed in a later chapter.) When Luther attempted to apply his emphasis on God's law to the structures of society, he found in that law divine sanction for a social order in which the ruler was to preserve law and order—with the sword, if necessary—while the pastor's function was the salvation of souls through Word and Sacrament.

This division of labor not only detached concern for justice from the province of the pulpit; it also prevented that concern from being the mandate of the public official. When the government's role in an oppressive society is to maintain law and order, it cannot advocate the kind of change that is needed to bring about justice. Instead, it must devote itself to the status quo. In Germany, the upper class civilian lived in two different kingdoms; the magistrate, in particular, had it both ways. He could come to church and be assured of an easy conscience, thanks to the grace of God proclaimed there, while during the week he was free, even compelled, to run a tight ship and keep society on its tried and true course. The very injustice in the world that might impose a sense of guilt or responsibility upon his soul was sustained by the gospel that took the pangs away.

For the German peasants it was an entirely different situation. Their weekday kingdom was one of misery. For centuries they had been waging a losing battle for life and basic human rights. When the gospel began to reach their ears, they sensed liberation, not from sin alone, but from economic enslavement as well. A God of grace could hardly have intended them to live forever on earth beneath the boot of landowners. Although life was a constant round of humiliation, the gospel conveyed a sense of worth: Sustained by the "armor of God," they peacefully brought their grievances to the attention of the prince. For reasons stated above, however, the prince was not predisposed to read the gospel the way the peasants did. He not only dismissed their grievances but, when a revolt ensued, ruthlessly put one hundred thousand of them to the sword. Luther was afraid to get involved publicly. The rise of these people from abject serfdom was set back hundreds of years. Consequently, in the early 1900s, Kaiser Wilhelm II found a people whose wings had been clipped, and from whose ranks the military could easily be filled.

TWENTIETH-CENTURY OVERTONES

Twenty years later, Adolph Hitler discovered the same thing. While he again prepared Germany for war there was barely a whisper of protest heard from the lips of either the laity or the clergy—and not because the pews were empty. A few individuals did raise their voices. One pastor, Dietrich Bonhoeffer, saw that there had been a great defection from God and Christ in the German church. He wrote that there were only two areas where God was still active and where the Church with its clergy was needed: death and guilt, both of which were on the border of life.[17] Most people still wanted a funeral conducted by the clergy, even though it was, at best, a fringe benefit. Those who went to church to receive forgiveness received it through the gospel proclaimed by the ordained preacher.[18] For most people, however, a God who showed little or no concern for the elimination or prevention of evil, who cared only about the pardoning of it, was difficult to believe in, for, as the war and its air raids reminded them daily, evil was a constant thorn in the side of humanity. For some this led to atheism. For others, it prompted the conclusion that God was separated from reality, that he had no connection with life.

For Bonhoeffer, the individualistic question of reaching heaven or gaining personal salvation had literally and theologically been blown to kingdom come. Moreover, he was struck by the fact that in the Old Testament the question about saving one's soul never appears.[19] Justice and the kingdom of God on earth are the motifs, the same two realities Jesus had said we were to place at the top of our list of priorities (Matt. 6:33). The God Bonhoeffer saw at work in Jesus was not on the edge of life but at its center, inseparably wedded to reality, though unrecognized as such.[20] In Jesus, God had revealed himself as the Man for Others. Therefore, "our relationship to God is not a religious relationship to a Supreme Being . . . but a new life for others, through participation in the being of Jesus."[21]

Thus, we see how in Germany the gospel had become emasculated over the centuries. It had no influence upon society and little on most of its citizens. The most God could do was wait for a few souls to come to pay him a visit in the church. Bonhoeffer, a Lutheran and an ardent admirer of the reformer, had a most interesting comment on Luther's desire that the clergy should remain aloof from the secular order. He believed, with one or two reservations, that had Luther been alive in the twentieth century he would have said the exact opposite on this question.[22]

Bonhoeffer was a voice, but, as with most prophets, his was one that issued from the wilderness of man's inhumanity to man and man's ignorance of God.

In America, where the Reformation had established a secure foothold, the situation was similar by the twentieth century. The gospel was boxed into a Sunday corner, unable to do much more than comfort victims and excuse their oppressors. For several centuries, for example, black people in America had drawn strength from Christ. They had become a suffering servant symbol, a national Christ figure, in their willingness to endure humiliation and hostility. Rather than attempt to lighten that burden, white society furthered itself, often at the black man's expense. Caucasian power not only used him to "tote that barge and lift that bale," but also used Jesus, albeit unwillingly, to keep the black man subdued.

The gospel has lost its power when those who profess to be Christ's followers seek him in a building in order to leave behind the world he loves, and to be assured that they are accepted "just as I am"—white, affluent, and middle class—while those same attitudes deny men and women in the community outside their human rights and confine them to a certain part of town. Redemption itself has turned sour when word and deed become enemies rather than friends. The subconscious message is that the truths Jesus and the prophets shared on the subjects of justice and peace are not meant to be taken seriously. It is as if the anticipated change in the individual, which comes from the impetus of Word and Sacrament, is supposed to affect the link with God but leave the relationship with others to shift for itself.

Thus far, this chapter has followed the course of the gospel in what has come to be called Christendom. It has not touched every event or every period, but rather highlighted some key eras and the thought prevalent in each. Taken together, these glimpses not only provide some perspective on our own times but, in doing so, say some very hard things to those of us who live in the West.

One is that accenting God's graciousness, or personal salvation, can and does lead directly to concerns that have been labeled "economic" and "political." This can be seen in the early Church at Jerusalem, where, in response to the gospel, the faithful pooled their material resources to eliminate poverty. It can be seen in the sixteenth-century German peasants' response to the gospel; for them it was, indeed, good news for the poor that led them straight to the door of economic-political power. It can be seen today in the migrant workers who, motivated by their Christian faith, have joined together to exert pressure on the growers.

Theoretically, the accent on what God has done for humanity in Christ should move all who hear of it to share these concerns. To say that the Church must commit itself to peace and social justice is, therefore, unnecessary. The founder of the Church has already so committed it through his own teachings, and he has urged its members to bear witness to God through social responsibility as well as through faith in divine forgiveness. Indeed, one who has had his personal needs met in the redemption of Jesus should be the first, not the last, to support the reform or renewal of society. Endowed with the love God has shown in Jesus, he has a sublime reason to be his brother's brother, unconditionally.

Moreover, what Luther's emphasis on faith in God's grace did was to liberate man from thinking that this life is a proving ground for the next. He can be free from anxiety about heaven, free to be open to what is going on around him on earth. With his eternal destiny provided for through Christ, the only world left to confront is this one. With his faith shaped by the friendship of God, a new set of concerns can be received, a view of economic need seen.

If history since the Reformation tells us anything, however, it is that the socio-economic implication in God's graciousness has remained just that, an implication. It rarely found its way into the pulpit, to say nothing of the pew. From the pulpit issued a steady diet of personal salvation, which many a layperson found quite acceptable—especially during Lent when the lights would be turned down low for evening services and all could survey the wondrous cross together. Winning souls for Christ took place in church, but in the world on Monday the parishioner confronted another reality, where business was business and profit was king. With faith and love separated, nobody, except for a voice in the wilderness like that of Walter Rauschenbusch, realized that our economic system espoused the opposite of what Christ taught, that getting ahead at the expense of the next fellow was incompatible with bearing one another's burdens.[23]

The traditional emphasis on salvation from this world was no help in meeting the challenge of the Industrial Revolution. And since the clergy lived in a world apart, the preacher seldom found out what effect our economic system in America had on the gospel he proclaimed from the pulpit. Now we know through various surveys taken on lay comprehension of the gospel that very little of what has been shared by the preacher was heard or applied to the everyday world of the working layperson.[24] Actually, our socio-economic system built within us an immunity to the impact of the gospel itself. When we work and sweat all through the week to earn a living, it is very difficult to believe what we hear in church, or to see how it fits into life from eight to five. When profit and economic competition motivate one five days a week, it is not easy to truly believe that, in relation to God, it's all done for us. The thought that Christ paid for our sins on the cross is almost impossible to reconcile with our daily situation, where we have to pay for everything ourselves. The heavenly reward for faith is too good to be true, or so far off the benefits do not compare with the opportunities for getting a new car, TV, or refrigerator.

Were cooperation and mutual concern rather than competition to become our economic priorities, it would become possible to recognize the God of the Bible at work in our midst. As it is, the popular belief today is in a religious God who must remain aloof from worldly affairs, but who meets us, we trust, once a week in church where he forgives us and nourishes us with the hope of post-mortem bliss.

What is at stake in all this and what is in the process of being redeemed by a growing number of voices in the wilderness is the credibility of God and the gospel. There are, indeed, two sides to the gospel, and both sides, not just one, must be redeemed from offense. Each needs the other. Faith needs love to avoid shutting man out, and love needs faith to avoid shutting God out. And the reason both are part of the gospel is that God is as much dedicated to the fulfillment of love as to faith. And there is no love without justice for the oppressed, be it in pharaoh's Egypt, Luther's Germany, or King's Alabama.

The issue is indeed that of the credibility of God and his gospel. During a time when hardship and misery are a way of life for a group or for the majority, the thought of heaven may serve a good purpose. The vision of eternity may be the one thing that keeps people going. Religion may keep alive, in the form of an idea, the values that man cannot realize in fact. However, when these values become realizable, it is an evil to keep such a "good" in "another world." When the needs of people can be met here and now, then a religion that does not support such endeavor is reactionary and debilitating.[25] In short, it is so heavenly minded, it is no earthly good.

The conclusion of this chapter, and an anticipation of the next, must be a response to the question this treatment of history begs, the question which is the theme of this book: What does God do when his Word is distorted and some people suffer because others refuse to yield the right of way? The answer to this query is seen on the cross. That lonely spot outside Jerusalem gives a clue as to what happens when someone dares to challenge those who control tradition and the purse strings without sufficient human support. When this happens, God as well as man suffers. And until the pressure of events can be brought to bear upon the situation, apparently the Creator of life must content himself with sustaining the spirit of those who are held down and with periodically raising up leaders to challenge both the strong and the weak, the rich and the poor, to lower the mountains and fill in the valleys.

ISSUES FOR DISCUSSION

1. Communal sharing in the first century was inspired by the spirit and teaching of Jesus.

2. A heaven-earth relationship underlies the traditional understanding of the Christian drama of salvation.

3. When Christ did not return, where he had gone took on ultimate importance.

4. One who has had personal needs met in the redemption of Jesus should be the first, not the last, to support social justice in society.

5. The separation of faith from love had no relationship to the development of a clergy and a laity.

6. What is needed is first to change the individual and then the system will take care of itself.

7. A popular view in the Church today is that the preacher's job is to save souls.

8. To keep a group of people down is to keep God at a distance.

9. The adage "business is business" is in opposition to the teachings of Jesus about concern for others.

10. When religion refuses to show an active concern for the poor, it is more evil than good.

NOTES

1. See Acts 2:46–47; 1 Cor. 11:20. The model for this was no doubt the Lord's Passover celebration in conjunction with the bread and wine of the Sacrament.

2. Acts 2:44–45; 4:32–37. Johannes Weiss notes that "higher values forced anxiety over property completely into the background." In place of a gnawing, crushing concern over their lot, they had a "confident trust in the heavenly Father" *(The History of Primitive Christianity* [New York: Wilson-Erickson, 1937], pp. 75–76).

3. James 2:1–7. James was also a leader in the Jerusalem church.

4. See 1 Cor. 13:13; Gal. 3; Eph. 2:28; Rom. 1:17, 3, 4.

5. See, for example, Joachim Wach, *Sociology of Religion* (Chicago: University of Chicago Press, 1944), pp. 138–42.

6. Acts 1:9–11. The vertical location of God's heavenly throne was well established in the Hebrew mind, thus making the ascension a communicative necessity.

7. See, for example, Rev. 7:9–17.

8. In Matt. 24:34–36 Jesus promised to return within that generation, though he admitted not knowing the exact time.

9. It took about ten years for Paul to move from the thoughts of 1 Thess. 4:15 to those in Phil. 1:20–25.

10. An intelligent lady in California, whose husband had just died, spoke of the camp song "You Can't Get to Heaven" as if it referred to a place up above, an image from which she sought to divest herself.

11. John T. Robinson, *Honest to God* (Philadelphia: Westminster Press, 1963), p. 15.

12. James A. Johnson writes that as the Church stressed the importance of gaining entrance to heaven, life on earth became relatively unimportant. Many viewed life on earth as nothing more than a means to a life hereafter, and with this the Western world plunged into the Dark Ages (James A. Johnson, et al., *Introduction to the Foundations of American Education* [Boston: Allyn and Bacon, 1971], p. 207).

13. Edward Gibbon, *The Decline and Fall of the Roman Empire* (Boston: Phillips Sampson & Co., 1852), 4:487. Speculation reached such proportions that it was pondered whether Christ's nature was "conflated," "conglutinated," or "coogmentated" (See E.C. Blackman, *Biblical Interpretation* [Philadelphia: Westminster Press, 1957], p. 110).

14. Jaraslov Pelikan, ed., *Luther's Works* (St. Louis: Concordia, 1958), 14:258.

15. Roland H. Bainton, *Here I Stand* (Nashville: Abingdon-Cokesbury Press, 1950), p. 65.

16. Martin Luther, *A Commentary on St. Paul's Epistle to the Galatians* (Philadelphia: Quaker City Publishing House, 1875), p. 225.

17. Dietrich Bonhoeffer, *Letters and Papers from Prison* (New York: Macmillan, 1972), p. 326. (The translation incorporates the text of the third English edition produced by Reginald Fuller, Frank Clarke, and others.)

18. The Reformation had succeeded in shifting the emphasis from the altar to the pulpit, from the eucharistic action of the priest to the homiletical word of the preacher.

19. Bonhoeffer, *Letters and Papers*, p. 286.

20. *Ibid.,* pp. 282, 312.

21. *Ibid.,* p. 381.

22. *Ibid.,* p. 123.

23. In *The Righteousness of the Kingdom* (Nashville: Abingdon, 1968), p. 233, Raushenbusch wrote that the London masses in 1912 on a Sunday morning were in the streets or parks talking, lying on the grass, eating oranges, while the well-dressed elite were going to churches and chapels.

24. By a two to one margin, 4,775 Lutheran listeners to sermons on what God had done for us in Christ affirmed in a survey that the main point of the gospel is in obeying the commandments (Merton P. Strommen, et al., *A Study of Generations* [Minneapolis: Augsburg, 1972], p. 369).

25. See Wilfred Cantwell Smith, *Modern Islam in India* (Lahore: Sh. Muhammad Ashraf, 1963), p. 125. Although Smith is speaking about modern Islam in India, his analysis of the thinking of Iqbal, an Islamic leader, is apropos for us as well.

CHAPTER 3

The Tragic Necessity of Karl Marx

Neither defenders nor foes of Karl Marx like to admit that his visionary theorizing was both tragic and necessary. Most capitalists and many Christians readily agree that it was a tragedy, but they see no reason why it was necessary. They point to parades of missiles in Red Square, children taken from parents at an early age, and the rise of an atheistic creed to support their view. Socialists and communists quickly agree that it was necessary, but do not admit the tragedy. To their minds come the upper classes' unwillingness to share their economic privileges and a religion that has poisoned human initiative and avoided the issues of this life.

Actually it was both a tragedy and a necessity. As the last chapter explained, religion itself, not Karl Marx, undermined faith in God and love for people. Marx merely put into words what many were feeling in his day—and ours. Indeed, it is the unwillingness of the poor to accept injustice that gives popularity and strength to the ideas of Marx. Originally, Christianity had had a solidarity with oppressed people. In its earliest stage it, too, had found communism a fitting social form through which to express its faith and life. What Karl Marx has done is to challenge humanity to regain this dimension, to encourage the longing for justice.

Communists are by no means the only ones who would agree that Marx was a necessity. In 1948 the World Council of Churches noted that it was one of the most fateful facts in modern history that often the working classes came to believe that the churches were against them or indifferent to their plight.[1] In 1969, Julius

Nyerere, president of Tanzania, wrote: "The churches in the developed countries have so far been on the side of the privileged, the powerful, and the rich, leaving alleged atheists to champion the cause of the oppressed, the poor, and the powerless."[2]

The Church had lost hold of its original charter, and an atheist had picked up the slack. Of particular relevance to the theme of this book is why Karl Marx was moved to do this, and where this puts him in relation both to God's announced priorities and to God himself.

A BAPTISED LUTHERAN

Karl Marx was born in Trier, Germany, in 1812. His Jewish parents both came from rabbinical families. This, however, did not prevent the elder Marx from having the entire family baptized as Christians in the Lutheran church. To hear that Karl Marx was baptized will surprise many Americans, including some Lutherans, but it is, nonetheless, a fact. The reason for this action, however, according to social scientist Francis Randall, is spurious. "Eventually," writes Randall,

> when Karl Marx was six, his father had himself and his whole family baptized as Lutherans not because he admired Luther or believed in Jesus, but to save his career in what was officially Lutheran Prussia, although Trèves [Trier] itself was a Catholic city.[3]

Taking Randall's words at their face value, they contain a contradiction. If Trier was a Catholic city, Marx senior hardly helped his law practice in the nineteenth century by becoming a Lutheran. That he did become a Lutheran in a Catholic city suggests more authenticity than career protection. As to the elder Marx's lack of admiration for Luther and belief in Jesus, one wonders how Randall learned of this. Given Lutheran Prussia, it would be a rather dangerous admission to make, especially if his career was at stake.

Randall would have the world think Marx and his son were above any religious background or influence.[4] Were such scholars as Randall to do their homework, however, without anti-religious bias, they would discover that young Marx not only attended a secondary school in which religion was taught, but that his schoolmaster also wrote the following on his "certificate of maturity":

His knowledge of Christian dogma and ethics is fairly well founded; he also is familiar with, in some measure, the history of the Christian Church.[5]

Moreover, Karl's father was not without religious inclinations. He frequently corresponded with his son when the latter went to college and on one occasion wrote these words to his offspring:

That you will remain morally good I really do not doubt. However, a great help for morality is pure faith in God. You know that I am anything but a fanatic. But this belief is for man sooner or later a real need; and there are moments in life in which even the atheist is involuntarily drawn to the adoration of the Highest.[6]

One cannot know whether the elder Marx was aware of the Lutheran doctrine of prevenient grace when he used the words "involuntarily drawn."[7] It can safely be assumed, however, that neither he nor the family had received baptism in Prussia without instruction in the Lutheran understanding of the Christian faith. Prussia was the leading Lutheran territory on the continent at that time, and provision for a clergy and for church services was carefully observed.

What the senior Marx meant by "anything but a fanatic" is not known either, but it is unlikely that he meant the policy, so common in the United States today, of ignoring participation in Word and Sacrament—especially if he was concerned about his career. He may have been alluding to the observance of family prayer, which was a private affair. Attending church, however, was a public occasion, and in Prussia it would have been a way of convincing a suspicious community that the conversion from Judaism had been genuine.

It could very well be that Karl's father felt pressure to become a Lutheran. However, since Randall offers no documentation for his statement, it remains an assertion in need of a source. Be that as it may, it is simply inaccurate for him to imply that the parents of Karl Marx had no beliefs with which to influence their son. Marx's Judeo-Christian background cannot be dismissed as of no account. Even the fact that Marx married the daughter of a Lutheran minister should not be overlooked. Long before then, however, his theistic orientation at home and exposure to Scripture in church school would at least have given him the feeling that there was order and design in nature, that human beings have value, and that there is a direction in history. Moreover, modern psychology destroys any notion that his parents had no influence upon him during his formative years. It is like saying that a person is raised in a vacuum. Parents transmit ideas and impressions to children by words, attitude, and example, whether consciously intended or not. We know this to be so today, and it was no different one hundred years ago. It is the perspective, not the experience, that has changed.

Proof of conscious influence, however, can come from only one authority, Karl Marx himself. Such proof is available. There is sufficient evidence that he took his exposure to his Judeo-Christian heritage seriously in his early years. From a final examination paper an essay has been preserved entitled, "Observations of a Young Man on the Choice of a Life-work." In it he expressed the following thoughts and phrases:

To men God gave a universal aim—to ennoble mankind and oneself. Each person has in view an aim which to him at least seems great, which is also important for all, if the deepest conviction, the innermost voice of the heart calls it that, for the Deity does not leave mortals entirely without a guide; it speaks quietly but sure.[8]

In a letter to his father in 1835, a most significant thought appears, similar to what today characterizes many members of the new generation throughout the world. "Before all things," he wrote, "I experienced here the disturbing influence of that opposition between what is and what ought to be which is the special character of idealism."[9] If there is any indication that Marx took his heritage seriously, it is in such a statement. Many adults today view idealism as a passing fancy, a phase, something out of which their offspring will one day grow. For countless young people, though, if religion does not influence what people say and do, it is mere verbiage; the words "peace," "love," and "God" are drained dry of meaning, for man does not live in a church, he lives in the world. This is the way Karl Marx felt at the age of seventeen when, for him, the difference between what is practiced and what is professed stood out in bold relief.

About this time his father died; with his passing other influences on the young Marx began to make themselves felt. But in a letter to his father just prior to the latter's demise, there is this parting thought concerning the concept of the Deity in religion, nature, and history:

> . . . I consider my position, in the same way as I look on life altogether, as the embodiment of a spiritual force that seeks expression in every direction in science, in art, and in one's own personality.[10]

THE DISILLUSIONED STUDENT

Against this theistic backdrop the atheistic reputation of Karl Marx may seem perplexing, but the age in which he lived and the circles in which he moved illuminate it. His transition from believer to atheist was not without cause, and it did not happen overnight.

Shortly after death closed the correspondence with his father, a new chapter opened in the life of Marx. At the age of twenty he was invited to join a club of professors at the University of Berlin, where discussion waxed hot and heavy on various issues. One of these topics was the recently published *Life of Jesus* by David Strauss.[11] What made this book so controversial was that in it Strauss had approached the study of the gospels with the same probing eye a scholar might use in secular biographical research on Napoleon, Lincoln, or John Kennedy. The result was that he portrayed Jesus merely as a human being; more important, he stated that the gospel record included legendary or mythological, as well as historical, elements. Today this is a common analysis of the gospels. Then it had the effect of a sledgehammer being applied to a foundation.

Another member of the university "doctors' club" was Bruno Bauer; he was nine years older than Marx, but he appreciated the latter's keen mind and realized that he was quite willing to consider more than one aspect of an intellectual question. In those circles at that time, religion was the "in" subject, and Bauer made the most of it because he was in the process of formulating his own bombshell, a book that demolished the ruins that Strauss had left standing. Published in 1841, *The Historical Criticism of the Synoptic Gospels* set forth the notion that everything in the gospels was the product of fantasy, and that Christianity itself was but a natural development of the Greco-Roman world. "In the prophecy as well as in the fulfillment," Bauer contended, "the Messiah was only an ideal product of religious consciousness. As an actual given individual he never existed."[12]

The young Marx was particularly vulnerable to these ideas. Just being invited to join this club was unusual, for he was not a professor nor had he yet written his doctoral dissertation. Nevertheless, he very quickly became the center of the group, and having reputable scholars pick his brains at such an early age no doubt flattered his ego and kept his thoughts on the same wavelength as those of his esteemed colleagues.

In the same year—1841—another book appeared on the scene, adding grist to the dialog. A simple, modest, ex-theological student, Ludwig Feuerbach, recorded his beliefs for posterity under the auspicious title *The Essence of Christianity,* and the effect on the Berlin group was, as Engels later said, "We all became Feuerbachians."[13] What Bauer did with Jesus, Feuerbach did with God. The only existence God had, he proposed, was in the mind of man, and he was there as a result of human reason and human wants. "God is the alter ego of man, what man ideally wants to be."[14]

Man is accused by his conception of God; he is judged and condemned. However, according to Feuerbach, man delivers himself by a consciousness of love, which forgives him, so that what he lacks in himself he enjoys more fully in his God. This redemptive invention took place in the first century when, for some reason, man was moved to contemplate God as a human being, and to surround this mental incarnation with an historical context—a life, a death, and a resurrection—for only in the presence of a flesh and blood person could man believe that a true, authoritative revelation had occurred.

To really appreciate the effect of Feuerbach on Marx, it is necessary to know something about the style and tone of the book. The first half reads like a devotional classic; at times the author gives the impression that he is affirming his own faith in God and Christ.[15] He presents Christianity as a psychological phenomenon, but constantly uses biblical language to do so; thus the effect on the unsuspecting reader can be misleading. The author shifts the basis of faith from God to man, from theology to anthropology, but it comes across as if he is communicating a new faith with the old vocabulary. For the young Marx this was particularly meaningful. He could read Feuerbach, moving freely in the biblical content he knew as a youth, and, at the same time, receive what seemed to be a new insight into the origin of faith. Since Bauer's book utterly destroyed faith, Feuerbach was therapeutic if not actually constructive. No wonder they all became Feuerbachians. He seemed to justify faith on new grounds, and there is evidence that Marx did the same thing. Later when he spoke of religion as the "opium of the people," he wasn't really denigrating it, but seeing it as a tragic necessity. Given the conditions under which the masses were living, it was the "sigh of the oppressed creature."[16]

Feuerbach also appealed to Marx because he addressed himself to the very problem that so troubled the young man: the gap between what Christians professed and what they practiced. When Feuerbach surveyed the religious landscape in the 1840s he saw little evidence of the kind of impartial concern that one would associate with the word "love." Instead, he saw what was described in the last chapter, a love that was tangled up with what passed for faith. Christian love had become narrow and exclusive. It related to people who believed the same way, but somehow it did not get beyond those who shared the faith. The Church had become a kind of lodge where care was shown to members, not to outsiders. Rather than being a bond between human beings, faith seemed to cut love short; faith truncated love. In the name of Christ heretics were damned and unbelievers consigned to hell.

The presence of such thought in the New Testament did not make it easier for Feuerbach—or Marx—to accept it. Faith focused attention on God, but since neither faith nor God were prompting genuine love, he concluded that God existed nowhere but in man's imagination as the enthronement of our pride and prejudice.

As Feuerbach saw it, faith was alienating man from himself and from others, and he wanted to liberate man from the bigotry and the superstition that he believed caused it. Rather than having men project themselves onto a God, he wanted them to see what was already theirs. His words were a manifesto to humanity, telling man that his desires could be satisfied here below, and by himself.

Few today would quarrel with his assessment of the need for love. Marx certainly did not. Today, however, Feuerbach's view of the origin of Christianity prompts certain questions.

What source of inside information led him to explain God in strictly psychological terms? If God's existence depends on man's mental exercise and is a product of it, why are men so unaware of this process? Why was nobody aware of it for 1800 years? Why did this inventiveness of the mind occur in the first century? Why were people moved to imagining God in human form at that particular time and in that particular place?

Questions such as these never occured to Karl Marx because his mind was predisposed to accept Feuerbach's ideas; the ground had been well cultivated by his conversations with Bauer. Moreover, it was a standing rule among contemporary philosophers, as one of them indicated, that they would not ask questions to which they had no answer.[17]

THE INSPIRED ECONOMIST

What did occur to Karl Marx, however, was the need to relate what Feuerbach said to what was going on in the world economically. Both men were intellectuals, but within Marx something more was brewing, something that directed him to say concerning Feuerbach: "Philosophers have only interpreted the world differently, the point is to change it."[18] What this something was, emerged in another statement Marx made, about the cultural impoverishment of the masses: "The needy man burdened with cares, has no appreciation of the most beautiful spectacle."[19] Whereas to David Hume, an eighteenth-century atheist, the masses were "vulgar,"[20] from Marx they elicited sympathy and pity, prompting one of his biographers to write: "God had burdened him with a heart which caused the common sorrow of humanity to touch him more acutely than others."[21]

All people looked at the same thing, but not all saw the same thing. To Marx much of society had given up. Amidst his economic theory in *Capital,* Marx vividly described the kind of cares that burdened the masses. Dwellings occupied by the working force in mid-nineteenth century urban England, where Marx lived, were dark, damp, dirty, stinking holes, utterly unfit for human habitation; they were badly supplied with water, and worse with privies.[22] In Newcastle-on-Tyne, 34,000 people lived in single rooms. In Bradford, a section from a "collecting agent's" list read as follows:

Vulcan Street, No. 122	1 room	16 persons
North Street, No. 17	1 room	13 persons
Jowett Street, No. 56	1 room	12 persons
George Street, No. 150	1 room	3 families
George Street, No. 128	1 room	18 persons
George Street, No. 130	1 room	16 persons
Edward Street, No. 4	1 room	17 persons
Salt Pie Street (bottom)	2 rooms	26 persons[23]

Many of these rooms had no beds. Occupants slept in their work clothes, on the bare boards, or with rags or shavings for a mattress. In Lancashire, it was a common tradition that the beds never got cold. Due to the practice of "night-working," facilities for sleep were used round the clock.[24]

The above was in stark contrast to the upper classes and monarchs who lived off the enormous profits, and the few middle-class folks who owned their own homes.

Ironically, the Church contributed to this social structure by teaching the proletariat to be patient and by comforting them with the hope of heavenly reward. All around him Marx found that people with little to hope for in this life were sustained by the thought of a better one beyond the grave. It was this kind of thinking that prompted him to see religion as a narcotic that helped people live with or escape from reality. Unable to have their pie on earth, the poor had to be content with the promise of it by and by in the sky.

It was here that Feuerbach's influence on Marx became crucial. He made it possible for Marx to focus his concern on the situation in this world rather than wait until the next. Taking the idea that human need had created God, Marx preoccupied himself with the socio-economic conditions that fostered the need in the first place. Indeed, Feuerbach was not just a foundation on which to stand, he became a threshold from which to step. At this juncture Marx took a curious exception to Feuerbach's emphasis. Rather than attacking the heavenly idea of equality, Marx felt that it was the earthly situation of inequality that should be eliminated, and he found a source of inspiration in the biblical image. "The criticism of heaven transforms itself therewith into the criticism of earth."[25] He was moved to make this his model for the kind of society that should exist on earth. Thus he used what he believed was an illusion—the kingdom of heaven—as the criterion by which an evil condition on earth was to be judged and corrected.

The question to which this leads—and it is of utmost importance to the theme of this book—is why an illusion held such fascination for Karl Marx? Of course, some psychologists believe that when misery and inner turmoil reach a certain level they give birth to dreams and visions. This theory may have some validity in this case, taking into consideration the fact that for years Marx lived in London in the kind of squalor his friend described above and that during those lean years two of his daughters died from malnutrition.[26] But even if this theory is true for Marx, it does not explain the particular content that took shape in his mind. The question remains.

Theologically he had been deeply influenced by Bauer and Feuerbach, but obviously something told him to relocate this paradisaic image of a free and equal society rather than discard it. A drastic bit of surgery had been performed on the meaning of Scripture, but the spirit was not so easy to remove. It fit too well into his own. He had left home and church when he went to the university, but there was a residue from those years that remained with him. Perhaps this was one of those moments in life, to which his father had semi-prophetically pointed, when "even the atheist is involuntarily drawn to the adoration of the Highest."

It would be a natural follow-through to contend that Marx had, in effect, borrowed ideas from the Bible without giving credit to its author. The case for this has been advanced by others, and, to be sure, one must seek the source of his vision in other than the society around him. It is really quite amazing that he was able to see a dynamic at work in the masses when one recalls the hopeless, static, and distressing conditions in which they lived. If he had seen this promise in an age of technological abundance, such as ours, it might be explainable, but coming out of the dark decades of industrial feudalism, one naturally wonders who turned on the light. Hegel and Feuerbach were influential, but Marx added very original insights. Scripture contained the light, but given his disposition toward it, one needs more than the pages on which it was printed to understand what motivated Karl Marx. One needs more than the residue to understand why it was something to which he was "involuntarily drawn." One needs more than the heart; one needs that reason the heart demands when the mind has ceased to be inquisitive.

A starting point is already provided in Fulton's reference to Marx's feeling for the poor as being God-given. He so designated it because one cannot say that such an inclination is native to all human beings, any more than is an interest in music, medicine, or meat cutting. The fact that one person has a propensity for one thing and another for another suggests that humankind has a variety of talents or gifts, that such are loaned to individuals for the benefit of the human family. But this explanation supposes a Giver. One can no more have a gift without a giver than a design without a designer. "If nature evinces wisdom, the wisdom is Another's" for nature has no intelligence with which to design anything.[27] The alternative to theism (or deism) at this point is coincidental design, not a very satisfactory substitute.

I would go further, however, in making a case for the theistic origin of Marx's motivation by asking whether it is possible to borrow something from God. Are not terms such as loan and gift a bit inappropriate, for we are not talking about a neighbor who loans us a lawnmower, or a colleague from whom we borrow a book, or a friend who gives us a gift. The Giver in this case is not one who lives in the house next door, but One in whose presence we all live; as Paul quoted from the Athenian poets, "in him we live and move and have our being" (Acts 17:26). If we receive something from him he cannot detach himself from it except by letting us *think* that it is ours. Were he to cease sustaining us and all that we have, the world and everything in it would cease to function. We may think that we get along well without him, but that is illusion. In the case of the sympathy Marx had for the poor, and the pull that he felt from the Spirit of the New Testament, we are dealing with just such a source of inspiration, a Source toward whom and by whom all people are at times "involuntarily drawn."

It would seem reasonable to conclude, on the basis of both the evidence of which Karl Marx was conscious and that of which he was not conscious, that he was not reacting merely in a human fashion to the conditions he witnessed in the world around him, but that he was also employed in the Lord's service. A corrective was necessary in order to refocus those who professed faith in God onto the priorities that he had originally born witness to through the prophets and his Son. The corrective God used was the vision of Karl Marx. In other words, the relationship between Marx and God might be described by the term *symbiosis*—a situation in which two dissimilar organisms find it necessary or advantageous to form a close association with one another.

The influence of Karl Marx on the priorities of justice and love can hardly be minimized. He may not be a household word, but he has the unchallengeable distinction of having set ideas in motion that have become a movement directly affecting the lives of most of earth's citizens. Some countries may claim to be apolitical, or to remain nonaligned, but they cannot avoid being affected by world politics, if only economically. Moreover, industrialized societies—no matter how much they claim to be based on pure capitalism—are, in fact, taking on more and more of the mechanisms of the socialist state, thereby suggesting that the ideas of Marx cannot be contained.

ISSUES FOR DISCUSSION

1. The Judeo-Christian tradition was a direct influence on Karl Marx.

2. The waning of idealism among adults results from a lack of faith in God's activity.

3. The poor who refuse to accept injustice are basically greedy.

4. Marx was God's instrument for drawing the attention of humanity to those left behind in the Industrial Revolution.

5. If nature evinces wisdom, it is the wisdom of Another, for nature has no intelligence with which to design anything.

6. There are times when we are all involuntarily drawn to the "adoration of the Highest."

7. The God Marx lost faith in, whom the masses believed in, did not exist except in their own minds.

8. Marx and Feuerbach were hypercritical in reacting negatively to the religious climate of their day.

9. Marx was more in harmony with the real God than he knew.

10. It is not possible to borrow something from God.

NOTES

1. *Findings and Decisions,* World Council of Churches First Assembly, Geneva, 1948, 1:87.

2. *Ecumenical Press Service,* no. 28 (July 31, 1969), p. 6. Nyerere related this when interviewed by an Urban Industrial Mission Advisory Group of the World Council of Churches, July 22, 1969, at the capital in Dar es Salaam.

3. Karl Marx, *The Communist Manifesto,* Introduction by Francis Randall (New York: Washington Square Press, 1971), p. 9 (original English edition 1888).

4. *Ibid.,* pp. 9–11.

5. *The Marx-Engels Collected Works,* ed. D. Ryazanov and V. Adoratskij, trans. Robert B. Fulton (Berlin: Marx-Engels & Lenin Institute, 1927–1932), I, ½, p. 183. Hereafter referred to as *Collected Works.*

6. *Ibid.,* p. 186.

7. "Prevenient grace" pointed to God's work within us preparing the way for faith before we realize he is doing so.

8. *Collected Works,* I, ½, p. 167.

9. *Ibid.,* p. 215.

10. *Ibid.,* p. 214.

11. David Strauss, *The Life of Jesus,* trans. George Elliot (London: Allen, 1913; first published in Leipzig: F.A. Brockhaus, 1864).

12. This quotation appeared in the original work on pages 14 and 247. It was quoted by Sidney Hook in *From Hegel to Marx* (New York: The Humanities Press, 1950), p. 91.

13. V. Adoratskij, ed., *Karl Marx, Selected Works* (New York: International Publishers, 1939), 1:427–28.

14. Ludwig Feuerbach, *The Essence of Christianity* (London: Ludgate Hill, 1881), p. 27. Translated into English by George Elliot (New York: Harper, 1957).

15. Nowhere does he say that the Christian is deceiving himself. That is, he doesn't use those words; but in one place he states that to think of the Incarnation as an "empirical fact" is "crass materialism" (*The Essence of Christianity,* p. 51).

16. *Collected Works,* 1:614–15.

17. Benedetto Croce said, "The questions to which philosophy has no answer have their answer in this, that they ought not to be asked." Quoted by William Chamberlain in *Heaven Wasn't His Destination* (London, 1941), p. 200. This is a book on Feuerbach.

18. An excellent treatment of this eleventh thesis on Feuerbach is given in Hook, *From Hegel to Marx,* pp. 303–07.

19. Quoted in Erich Fromm, *Marx's Concept of Man* (New York: Frederick Ungar Publishing Co., 1961), p. 134.

20. David Hume, *An Enquiry Concerning Human Understanding,* Harvard Classics (New York, Collier, 1910), 37:362 and 376.

21. Robert B. Fulton, *Original Marxism Estranged Offspring* (Boston: Christopher House, 1960), p. 71.

22. Karl Marx, *Capital,* trans. Samuel Moore and Edward Aveling (Chicago: Charles H. Kerr & Co., 1906), 1:726.

23. *Ibid.,* 1:727.

24. *Ibid.,* 1:832.

25. Marx, "Toward the Critique of the Hegelian Philosophy," *Collected Works,* 1, 614–15. This article, which was written in 1843 for the *German-French Yearbook,* includes several paragraphs on the subject.

26. These were years when Marx was busy writing, but very little was being published. He was a columnist for the New York *Herald Tribune,* but what he earned was not enough to live on.

27. Frank R. Tennant, *Philosophical Theology* (Cambridge: The University Press, 1930), 2:109.

CHAPTER 4

The Theological Left

I do not know why the conservative is always designated as being on the right and the liberal on the left, but I do know that both right and left have one thing in common: They must work to achieve their ends. What they differ on are the ends. The right works hard to keep things as they are, while the left is concerned with new life. Both have been known to employ violence, but the one has used it to prevent change, the other to effect it.

Few would disagree that Karl Marx is on the left. Remember that it was he who said, "Philosophers have only interpreted the world differently, the point is to change it."[1] Also on the left would be Amos, Isaiah, John the Baptist, and Jesus. Anyone interested in liberty and justice for the oppressed is on the left.

In speaking of a theological left, one thing must be clarified immediately. In the popular view God is unchanging, and even with regard to Jesus the Scripture suggests as much by saying he is the same yesterday and today and forever (Heb. 13:8).

I would agree that neither God nor Jesus Christ change in nature or objectives, but it can easily be demonstrated that this fact supports rather than suspends the need for change in human relationships. According to the Old Testament prophets and the New Testament Christ, God is dedicated to the liberation of the oppressed and to the reshaping of swords into plows. Thus, as long as people throw up roadblocks in God's path, he must work to remove them, or he ceases being true to himself.

What words to use in describing this activity of God is the main question of this chapter. Finding them will help clarify God's relationship to an atheist. It will also make more comprehensible the theme of the chapters ahead: the relationship of God's activity to modern persons and events.

In the last chapter I referred to Marx as the "inspired economist," but I described God's influence in passive terms. To say one cannot borrow from God because God is omnipresent does not suggest much activity on God's part. To say that Marx's feeling for the poor was God-given suggests a kind of latent capacity that is simply there and lingers for a lifetime. To say that the Spirit was left over from his youth hardly brings to mind divine initiative. Neither does the phrase "involuntarily drawn"; as important as it may be in understanding Marx, it has a rather localized connotation. In fact, it sounds like a magnet permanently stationed somewhere and sending out irresistible vibrations.

Describing God's active involvement in human affairs requires a different language and a different pattern of thought. In pursuing these objectives it is necessary to face squarely two issues that are currently confronting students in the field of philosophical theology, both of which have to do with the relationship of verification to faith.

INCOGNITO ACTIVITY

The first issue to be considered in describing the activity of God in the events and happenings of society is one of visibility or invisibility. Because God is unseen, to talk about his activity raises the very legitimate question as to how we know it exists. Of course God has already revealed his priorities through Scripture, but every age has its own questions; the question of verifying what is invisible is vital enough today to warrant further treatment here.

To arouse a feeling for this question, the reader is invited to consider a parable developed by Anthony Flew from a tale told by John Wisdom about two explorers who come upon a clearing in a jungle. Both flowers and weeds are growing in the clearing. One explorer says, "Some gardener must tend this plot." The other disagrees, "There is no gardener." So they pitch their tents and set a watch. No gardener is ever seen. "But perhaps he is an invisible gardener." At this they set up a barbed-wire fence. They electrify it. They patrol with bloodhounds. But no shrieks ever suggest that some intruder has received a shock. No movements of the wire ever betray an invisible climber. The bloodhounds never give cry. Still, the believer is not convinced. "But there is a gardener, invisible, intangible, insensible to electric shocks, a gardener who has no scent and makes no sound, a gardener who comes secretly to look after the garden which he loves." At last the skeptic despairs: "But what remains of your originial assertion? Just how does what you call an invisible, intangible gardener differ from an imaginary gardener or even from no gardener at all?"[2]

Believers in the New Testament can say with faith that the Gardener did visibly enter the garden 1,900 years ago. Then too, Wisdom's reference to weeds is pertinent: "An enemy has done this," Jesus related in a parable of his own.[3] But rationality also supports the believer. The empirical facts were the same for both men. Each saw what the other saw with the physical eye. The difference, nevertheless, is more than one of interpretation; weeds grow unaided, but flowers require lots of care (unless, of course, they are wild flowers, which is not a part of Flew's story). The issue is that something was happening in the clearing. One man was interested in why and, through his faith, found an answer. The other man had a faith, too, but found no answer through it. Even more to the point, he was little motivated to pursue the question. For both men the gardener was out of sight, but only one was moved to acknowledge it, even though the garden conveyed a message as to his presence. It was not a question of faith or no faith, but which faith and which response was appropriate to the empirical facts. Then, too, there is a difference between the terms *invisible* and *imaginary*. It is possible to have a garden cared for by an invisible gardener, but not by an imaginary one, or by none at all.

In spite of the believer's defense, however, it must be acknowledged that in our time the gardener does remain hidden. The first theologian to address himself to this aspect of God's relationship to what goes on in the world was Martin Luther. It wasn't the existence of the gardener that troubled him, but his purposes. Luther felt in his bones that it was wrong for the landlords to thrive while the lowly suffered, but he could not bring himself to say about the state what he so readily said about the Church: that those in positions of power can become corrupted. Rather he assumed that God was working through opposites to accomplish his purposes, that behind a frowning providence was hidden a smiling face.[4] Today we are not so naive about persons in leadership positions. We also know that the very structure of a society can perpetuate evil, a thought that even the foremost champion of liberty could not take seriously in the sixteenth century.

Today we also realize that it is logically impossible to say that there is a side to God that is unknown. To make such a statement the person doing so would have to have some inside information to that effect, which would render the unknown known—at least to him. William James was one of the first to see this. "Which part of my unknown self is in my awareness, which is out?" he asked. "If I name what is out, it already has come in."[5] Consequently, we can only know of God what he has revealed to us about himself, and we cannot say there is something about him that we do not know unless he has revealed this to be so.

Today, the empirical activity of God both supports faith, and in turn, is supported by it. What remains hidden is God himself. Carl Braaten, a modern Lutheran theologian, came close to expressing this when he observed that "God is the hidden pressure for justice in the world."[6] Actually it is not the pressure that is hidden, but the source of the pressure. However, God has been associated with heaven and the soul for so long that it is difficult to think of him involved in economics or politics, even though human efforts for justice and peace are priorities to which God has revealed a commitment. In other words, as far as faith is concerned, God has been removed from his office and has had to carry on his work in an unofficial manner without recognition or acknowledgment.

By way of application, the God Karl Marx lost faith in did not exist except in his own mind. The one and only God was actively at work in Marx's life and thought, the hidden pressure for justice to which Braaten referred.

An American illustration of this pressure began in Montgomery, Alabama, when Rosa Parks boarded a bus and paid her fare.

She was accustomed to riding the bus in the rear section assigned to black people, and when it was full she stood. It was full this time, but to initiate a reaction she sat down in the white section. She was weary as usual after cleaning Caucasians' houses, but this time she had support from two Kings, one seen, the other unseen. She had thought about sitting anywhere on the bus before, but fear had always prevented the thought from becoming an act. This time, however, courage joined her fatigue. She sat down and refused to yield her seat to a white man who requested it. Thus began the nonviolent activity on the part of blacks—and God—to gain a constitutional birthright. From all outward appearances it did not look like God was involved, at least not to the white citizenry. To them Rosa Park's action and the ensuing bus boycott were simply a case of "niggers" getting out of line, a revolt of the malcontents.

However, there is a historical precedent for believing that God is involved when most appearances are to the contrary. That is the precedent of Jesus Christ. During his three-year ministry only one person—Thomas—referred to him as God (John 20:28), and this no doubt would not have happened had not God intervened and raised Jesus from the dead. Jesus looked like a man, not a god or the God. He got tired. He perspired. He had to eat to stay alive.

He had to sleep to restore strength. Moreover, he was a Jew, a man from Nazareth, thought to be Joseph's son. God was unrecognized in this form, not just because he was thought to be comfortably enthroned in heaven above, but also because Jesus was so truly human that no one suspected he was the Creator's earthly counterpart.

To the eye of faith, God made known his ways in Jesus. But also included in this revelation was the pronounced inclination to let the person be a person. Jesus distinguished himself by unusual powers and concerns, but while, for some, these called attention to God, God's presence in Jesus was strictly incognito. The God whom we see in Jesus Christ is shy, unassuming, and reticent about identifying himself.

In other words, part of the witness that God makes to himself is to leave his witness to the response of those who are moved not by sight, but by faith, and who, therefore, honor him for his Word, without the need of spectacular manifestations.

It is in this area that the theological left has a contribution to make to our understanding of God. When we look for a way to put into words how God could enter into individuals and groups unrecognized, we find help in the language and thought of various theologians. One way of describing it appeared in the 1960s, when Thomas Altizer tried to put meaning into what he called the "death of God." He spoke of God undergoing a metamorphosis, the first sign of which he saw in Jesus' life.[7] He envisioned a process whereby God emptied himself into humanity, a process that involved the transfer of God's primordial life and power into humanity until he became as one unknown, a "lifeless nothingness" in the minds of people. Altizer saw this descent of the Unseen God into concrete human history as being only gradually realized by mankind, and the process continually moving forward to an eschatological end, a time when this hidden presence of God would be revealed.

Altizer is by no means alone in attaching universal significance to what happened in Jesus Christ. In 1963 the Vatican Council announced that "by his Incarnation the Son of God has united himself in some fashion with every man."[8] A few years later the World Council of Churches affirmed this kind of thought when it declared that "nothing is the same since the death and resurrection of Jesus Christ. In him a new creation has dawned."[9]

It is a timely insight to speak of what happened in Jesus as the inauguration of a new age in the human family, rather than as events in the history of one man only. It helps us think of Jesus as our contemporary. However, such statements taken by themselves can give the impression that in the wake of God's demise, Jesus is being asked to carry the freight that the deity once did. For many Jesus loses something when his connection with God is severed and he is supposed to make it on his own. Actually it is not necessary to theologize that God had to give up his primordial power in order to enter the human race. The "new creation" can be expressed in ways that include God. Eric Mascall, an English theologian, gave Christ this kind of theological support when he wrote, "In Jesus the Creator joined human nature to himself, and made it the medium of his own life."[10]

Another way of describing in words how God can be active, although unrecognized, participating in the lives of people and nations, is to say that in Jesus God reveals for those who are willing to look what his relationship with humanity is and always has been. In contrast to Altizer, I would say that the function of the Word is not to make God unknown, but to make him known. Rather than dying in Jesus, God thereby comes to life in him. Oddly enough, had Altizer wanted God to remain incognito, or had he wished our thoughts to remain untouched by his words, he should not have written about the "death of God." Once it had been put into words, it ceased to be a secret; what was concealed became revealed.[11]

In some theological circles today it is fashionable to speak of the absence of God. What the theologians are pointing to is his hiddenness, another insight of the theological left. However, if someone is hiding from us and we are told that this is what he is doing, then something of the hiddenness or absence has been removed; we at least know we must look for him. And if we are further informed as to his whereabouts, as we have been in Christ, then he is neither absent nor hidden any longer. Through the Word, God, in a sense, calls attention to himself. Through Jesus, God emptied himself in his human creation, and the New Testament writers were the first to give us this Word (see Phil. 2:5–11).

If you follow this thought, Jesus Christ becomes that point in history when the Unseen One came out of hiding long enough to disclose the direction of his activity and the nature of his relationship with humanity. Through Christ, God stepped from behind the curtain onto the stage of history and addressed all humanity by way of the segment that lived in Palestine nearly 2,000 years ago.

In the context of this book's theme, it does not matter whether the emphasis is on God revealing what he is doing in Jesus, or on his beginning something altogether new in Jesus. Either way, there is no broader or different foundation for individuals or society than God has revealed through Jesus. Neither Marx nor any other human being can activate something for the benefit of others in which God is not participating. Because of God and Easter the Incarnation continues, allowing us to believe that God is on the move from generation to generation, pursuing the path of least resistance or most response, as he seeks to instill a new humanity into the kingdoms of this world. In the words of Frederick Maurice, "We stand not in Adam but in Christ."[12]

THE NONEXPERIENCED PRESENCE

A corollary to God's incognito activity and to the relationship of verification to faith is that in everyday life we are not aware of either God or Christ within us or around us, even though our words may convey an impression to the contrary. We neither perceive God at work in the world, nor do we experience him within, even if we shut our eyelids and probe the inner recesses of our minds.

This is perhaps the main reason why Paul was moved to write so much about Christ being in us and about the Spirit supplying strength to the inner man.[13] Had he or his readers been living with an awareness of God or Christ that identified itself, there would have been no need for him to write about it. As it was, through Paul's words God was bearing witness to his incognito presence and activity. We are dependent upon the Word for our awareness.

Feuerbach was right in making man's awareness of God an issue, although he was wrong in the conclusions he drew. There is perhaps nothing today that can be more misleading than the realization of God that people have been taught to think they should have. (This was true in Paul's time also.) Our words say one thing, but our experience, if we examine it, says something quite different. So, unless our faith in Christ is well grounded in the Word, the little we have can be easily lost.

When someone writes a book or preaches a sermon on prayer, he customarily speaks not only of the words people direct to God but also of the fact that prayer entails listening to God. This used to puzzle me, because, try as I might, I never "heard" God speak to me or with me the way that expression led me to expect. When praying I knew most of the time that I was not talking to myself, but not once did God or Jesus appear to me empirically, subjectively, or in any way that assured me that he was listening, let alone that he was communicating with me in return.

An additional illustration may be in order. In the early 1960s I recall a visit to a Roman Catholic Mass, followed by a private huddle with the priest. A question that I put to him went something like this: "It would seem, at the moment when you elevate the host and the bell rings, signaling that Christ has entered the bread, that you would experience an overwhelming sense of his presence, that you would be conscious of Christ being very near. Is this so?" The priest's response astounded me, and, as I reflect on it now, the answer was all the more significant because had he wanted to put in a plug for Catholicism that would have been the time to do so. I would never have known otherwise. In a sense what he replied was reassuring. He said, "No, I really do not feel the presence of Christ at all. Perhaps it is because I say Mass so often, but for me there really is no awareness that he is present."

Now uninformed Catholic lay persons might say that this fellow was neither a priest nor a Catholic. On the other hand, it could be that he was speaking for every priest that ever said Mass, the difference being that he was prompted to reflect on his experience and put it into words. When he did so what came forth was the realization that the appearance is quite different from the experience itself, and hence misleading or misrepresentative. It is not that we intentionally deceive others by our words, but that we take our experience for granted and usually do not think about it.

The above illustrations took place in the privacy of the mind and of the church. However, what is true there is equally true in the home, in the street, in the office or factory. God is at work there too, but we are not aware of it experientially. We can be conscious of the pressure for peace, justice, and truth, but we cannot feel aware of the Source of this pressure. This nonexperienced presence, known through the Word alone, prompted Dietrich Bonhoeffer to express what at first seems like a contradiction. He wrote that God is at the center of life; yet so nonexperienced is this presence that he further wrote that God wants us to get along in the world as if we were "without him."[14] It would seem reasonable to assert that the only way in which one can be at the center of our existence and yet be that unknown to our consciousness is if he transcends us, not by being geographically above us, but by being interior to us.[15] Perhaps what Bonhoeffer was struggling with finds articulation in the thought of William James. After analyzing varieties of religious experience, he observed:

Every bit of us at every moment is part and parcel of a wider self. And just as we are co-conscious with our own momentary margin, may not we ourselves form the margin of some more really central self which is co-conscious with the whole of us? May not you and I be confluent in a higher conciousness, and confluently active there, though we now know it not?[16]

It is perhaps in such a way that Bonhoeffer could declare God to be central to all our experience yet experienced as if he were not there at all.

All this helps us understand how God can be at work in the life and thought of an atheist. It also explains why Feuerbach was right in suggesting that people are unaware of the origin of their ideas, but was wrong in concluding that people's mental images are all the products of their imaginations. In so doing he pulled the rug out from under himself. He who undermines everything undermines himself: He has no way of proving that his own ideas are not the product of his own imagining.

Moreover, when Feuerbach asserted that people fantasized the entire Incarnation because they wanted a God in tangible form, we know that he was the one laboring under an illusion. The New Testament makes it painfully clear that the historical process by which God made himself in man's image was beyond not only the belief or comprehension of Feuerbach, but that of many Palestinians as well. "He came to his own home and his own people received him not," John wrote, with one eye on the crucifixion (John 1:11). Rather than creating God in the image of Jesus, most of them rejected him. The message was God's kingdom priorities and his forgiveness, but, unfortunately, Jesus could not get this message through to the powers that be or to many of the people.

At this point Carl Braaten once again has words that are help-ful: "Man's consciousness of God is no index of his power or presence."[17] This is best illustrated in the life and experience of Jesus. As a man just over thirty he had grown sufficiently in wisdom to realize that the worship of God could occur anywhere through "spirit and truth" (John 4:23–24). He had not always believed this. When he was twelve he was convinced that God was located in the temple in Jerusalem—at least he referred to it as "my Father's house" (Luke 2:49). From this we might infer that for a number of years his consciousness of God's presence had been confined to a building in another town miles from where he lived. Yet, for eighteen years he had performed a ministry to the general public and his immediate family by working as a car-penter, presumably building and repairing furniture. He may not have been aware of God being in him or with him there, but such awareness was not necessary in order for him to render this service.

Although he was conscious of God being his Father, there is reason to believe that throughout his life he was more aware of being himself than of being the Father. John does record him saying, "He who has seen me has seen the Father" (John 14:9), but this can hardly refer to a physical identity. It must instead refer to an identity of activity or policy. Throughout his visible ministry Jesus talked to God as a person other than himself. Even on the cross he spoke in this fashion. This need not be interpreted to mean that God was not one with Jesus (or Jesus with God, for that matter), but rather that Jesus, being truly human, possessed a consciousness, as do we, and like ours it was intact as a self.

Jesus, wittingly or unwittingly, pointed to this issue of con-sciousness when he welcomed some people into his kingdom "for I was hungry and you gave me food, I was naked and you clothed me, I was sick and you visited me, I was in prison and you came to me." Those who heard this could not believe their ears. They were unaware of ever having seen Jesus hungry, thirsty, a stranger, cold, sick, or behind bars. Then he startled them even further by identifying himself with those people who were in such need and concluding, "As you did it to one of the least of these my brethren, you did it to me" (Matt. 25:35–40). When Jesus' followers had performed such service, they had only been conscious of human need, of the needs of others. They did not have the vaguest notion that they were doing this to him, until he told them.

That is the key point in this issue of our consciousness of God's incognito activity. A human being's awareness is not based on his feelings or spiritual temperature. It is based on faith, the content of which is supplied by the Word of God, both written and living. Words and words alone shape the human consciousness, and this includes awareness of God's power and presence. This awareness depends on the witness God bears to himself, a witness communicated through words.

It is for this reason that I said the objective of this chapter was to search for a language that would describe God's activity. There is no other way that human beings can become aware of it or of him. It is through God's promise to be with men that they can believe he hears them when they pray, not through an overwhelming sense of his presence or of his voice. It is through the statement "This is my body" that Catholics believe Jesus enters the host, not through an exhilarating experience of his nearness. And it is through Scripture that Christians can find and believe God to be at work in the so-called secular affairs of society. Once they realize that these affairs are witness to the Word, it becomes impossible not to see demonstrations of his activity in the reports of the media day by day.

The impression we Christians have conveyed by our solemn assemblies and proclamations of faith is that somehow God is favoring us with a presence unlike his presence to other people. However, in one sense we worship and believe "in name only." In God's name we gather. In his name we pray. But the ever-present need that we feel is as real to us as to the atheist. The difference is one the Word makes, as the Spirit through the Word implants and cultivates faith, thereby clarifying what we are experiencing.

ISSUES FOR DISCUSSION

1. Anyone interested in liberty and justice for all is on the "left."

2. The issue in the Gardener story is which faith do the empirical facts support.

3. We can only know of God what he has revealed of himself.

4. It is easier to think of God as divine than as human.

5. Rather than dying in Jesus, God came to life in him.

6. We cannot activate something for the benefit of others in which God is not participating.

7. Our words convey one impression about God's presence, but our experience conveys another.

8. Our consciousness of God is no index of his power or presence.

9. Awareness of God is based on his Word alone.

10. The difference between an atheist and a believer is not in their experience of God, but in their faith in his Word.

NOTES

1. Eleventh Thesis on Feuerbach.

2. Antony Flew and Alasdair MacIntyre, *New Essays in Philosophical Theology* (New York: Macmillan, 1964), p. 96.

3. Matt. 13:28. In Col. 1:15, Paul describes Christ as the "image of the invisible God."

4. See Bainton, *Here I Stand,* pp. 218, 241. Luther affirmed that the severities of God would one day be seen as his mercies.

5. William James, *A Pluralistic Universe* (New York: Longmans, 1909), p. 288.

6. Carl Braaten, *The Future of God* (New York: Harper, 1969), p. 95.

7. Thomas J. Altizer, *The Gospel of Christian Atheism* (Philadelphia: Westminster, 1966), pp. 103, 107–09.

8. Walter M. Abbott, *The Documents of Vatican II* (New York: America Press, 1966), pp. 208 and 221.

9. Norman Goodall, ed., *Uppsala 68 Speaks* (Geneva: World Council of Churches), p. 23.

10. Eric Mascall, *The Christian Universe* (New York: Morehouse, Barlow Company, 1966), p. 25.

11. Bonhoeffer did this also. He believed that God wants us to get along in this world without a consciousness of him. That is what the cross said to this theologian, but he was hardly content to keep it to himself.

12. *The Life of Frederick Dennison Maurice* (London: Macmillan, 1884), p. 358.

13. In his letters Paul speaks of living or being in Christ or of Christ being in us 164 times. For examples, see Gal. 2:20 and Col. 3:3.

14. Bonhoeffer, *Letters and Papers,* pp. 282, 360.

15. I am indebted to Edward Schillebeeckx for this thought. See *Revelation and Theology* (New York: Sheed and Ward, 1967), p. 116.

16. James, *A Pluralistic Universe,* p. 290.

17. Braaten, *The Future of God,* p. 95.

CHAPTER 5

God's Political Activity

Jesus did not demonstrate an interest in the political affairs of Rome, but this cannot be understood to mean that civil responsibility was beyond his realm, for two reasons. One, he was well acquainted with the writings of Isaiah that the earthly government was to rest on the shoulders of a Son, bearing the credentials of the God of Peace (Isa. 9:6–7). And two, he believed that a kingdom of peace would come in the first century (Matt. 24:34), so it was unnecessary to criticize Caesar.[1] He would soon be redeemed from the desire to oppress people and wage war anyway, through the intervention of God.

Although the kingdom did not collectively arrive in the first century, we do not see subsequent history in terms of Paul: God appointing public servants to function in his absence (Rom. 13:1–7).[2] They may function in his behalf, but not because God has abdicated his rule. And the Son can be at work even when officials are not receptive to his aims or are not pursuing them for worthy reasons.

This became apparent during the past ten years of American history, when certain persons in governmental positions were forced out of office or compelled to change their policy due to the pressure of truth. The United States revealed during the recent Vietnam trauma that its government is of, by, and for people, through whom God is at work, when for one of the few times in the course of history the brakes were put on a military effort because public opinion within the nation waging it turned against it.

How this came about belongs in this book because, seen in

relation to God's activity, Vietnam is far from the dark spot on our record that many make it out to be. Moreover, it is a unique example in modern times of how the pressure of truth can serve a political purpose, when for most folks politics is believed to be the arena of deception.

The vehicle for this pressure was that of the communications media, a media which for a democracy is both a strength and a weakness. It is a strength if what is printed as truth is in accord with the announced priorities of God, but if the news that a paper or a network deems fit to make known is not in accord with such priorities, then those readers or listeners are being misled. The possibility of distortion was confirmed in a case study on the selection of news, appropriately entitled "The Gatekeeper," in which it was found that an editor rejected nine-tenths of the news that came to his desk from the wire services, in part due to space, but mostly because the news did not agree with his point of view. Penciled in on the margins of the rejected news items were such reasons as "He's too Red," "Never use this," "B.S.," and "Propaganda," all of which presume prior criteria of judgment.[3]

What appears in this chapter as truth, and as God's way of bringing pressure to bear upon the powers that be, may very well be news to some readers, depending upon where they happen to live. Although the context of the chapter provides perspective, the news data will largely speak for itself, with the exception of the last section—the results of truth.

THE NEWS FROM 'NAM

When the United States moved into South Vietnam to liberate the people, it was not long before we learned that our presence there was no more appreciated than was that of the Soviet troops who entered Prague in 1968 to do the same thing.[4] In fact, a thirty-three year old South Vietnamese school teacher turned herself into a torch to protest it. In a letter written by her and delivered to the Associated Press in Saigon in 1967, she wrote:

You, the United States, have dropped so many tons of bombs and money on my people's heads, that it has destroyed their bodies and minds. Don't you know that in their inner self the Vietnamese people resent the Americans who have brought war to their country.[5]

Vietnamese men, who had to peddle their wives and daughters to American soldiers to supplement the family income, detested us; so did middle-class Vietnamese who could not find housing because landlords preferred renting to Americans who would pay outrageous sums without complaint.[6] Few Vietnamese civilians had the courage of the teacher, so they reacted in a way that our soldiers came to regard as the nature of the war. They were friends by day, but foes by night.

In Vietnam, as in Prague, the visiting militia were bewildered. GIs naturally wondered, "If these people hate us so, what are we doing here, so far from home?" They began to feel like the British troops during the American Revolution,[7] and they reacted in a way unprecedented in recent American history. There have always been those who "took off" during a war, but never before has the United States had to admit that in a single year the number of deserters and men absent without leave totaled ten divisions—155,000 men. (The Armed Services Committee reported that in 1968 this averaged out to one every three minutes.) In addition, the stockades were filled with men who had accepted the draft rather than face the stigma of that time by refusing it, but then responded to what they had seen and experienced by announcing themselves conscientious objectors.

In previous wars soldiers have, on occasion, fired over the heads of the enemy rather than at them, but never before have they painted peace symbols on their rifles and helmets. During World War I Allied and German troops exchanged coffee and cigarets in the trenches at night, then shot each other during the day. But in Vietnam the will to kill was more drastically undermined for many. "We were being ordered to kill young men we had never met, and with whom we had no quarrel," an infantryman said, "whereas the ones we wanted to do in were our own lieutenants, who demanded unnecessary risks."[8]

In 1968, four young South Vietnamese students at Harvard articulated their feelings. The four were grim-faced until it came to speaking about pacifying the villages by bulldozers and bombers in order to "win the hearts and minds of the people." This prompted a grin, for their country had become a theatre of the absurd, and the gap between our aims and our results was so wide it forced a smile.

"We want American help, but not military," said one of the four. "Your military help is like cutting off a head to cure cancer of the throat."

"You must stop the obliteration immediately and negotiate with the NLF and the North Vietnamese," said another.[9]

THE INITIAL RESPONSE

As this kind of news from the occupied country of Vietnam found its way to America, the reaction it produced was akin to an earthquake within and among people. The first to affirm the truth of what they heard was the student generation. The report from the Harvard four made *The Boston Globe* and helped kindle a fire among the area's many thousand collegians. For example, in Stockbridge, Massachusetts, a young man had to pay a fifty-dollar fine for dumping garbage in the wrong place. When soon thereafter he reported for his army physical, the army made one of its biggest mistakes. He was told to examine himself to see if he realized the error of his ways in Stockbridge. At that moment the "anti-massacre movement" was born in America. Arlo Guthrie just could not accept the idea that an armed force specializing in "burning women, kids, houses, and villages" was asking him, a litterbug, if he was morally rehabilitated. When the irony of this situation was set to music, it struck a chord that turned on a generation and made Alice's restaurant more than a song.[10]

Affirming the truth of the news was not limited to New England. In 1967 ten campus leaders—student body presidents and college newspaper editors—went to the microphone in the House Agriculture Committee hearing room to announce in stark but courteous terms their intention of refusing induction into the armed forces. These were articulate young Americans, the cream of the campus crop, who were willing to go to prison for love of their country. Other students, unable to contain their rage, vented it on the institution nearest at hand, the campus. Still others sought escape through drugs.

In California, the son of a retired Navy captain poured

kerosene over himself and lit a match. A sign hung on him said, "In the name of God end the war." Three years before he had been a ROTC student. To his mother "he was just too sensitive." He was not a radical. He was unaffiliated with any political group. He just could not see himself taking another person's life. Society was asking him to commit homicide, and the only way out he saw was suicide.[11]

Sensitivity is an apt word to describe what the young were experiencing, and it wasn't just because they were next in line to fill the ranks of the military. The young are usually more sensitive to the prevailing winds than their elders, and in the case of this new generation there had been several influences that combined to shape their consciences, making them receptive to the news from Vietnam.

One was the civil rights movement. Although some aspects of the move toward racial justice were stalled by the Vietnamese conflict, it did help put the brakes on the war. Student revulsion over cruelty had been nurtured in the South in the early sixties. And once young people had been sensitized to the dignity of the downtrodden and to the need to love, they could hardly be taught to kill, at least not willingly. (Considering the part violence has always played in the history of our country, this was no small miracle in itself.)

Documentation of the connection between the civil rights movement and the antiwar protest is available. One of the first white youths to refuse to register for the draft had spent a summer in the South and had become committed to nonviolence. "I believe," wrote Tom Rodd, "that it is far better to turn the other cheek, to accept suffering willingly, than to harm others. In this willingness to suffer I see the greatest power in the world: . . . love." Tom was unusually aware of the source of his courage and inspiration. Testifying on his own behalf before a Federal grand jury, he noted that even if the penalty were to be twenty-five years in prison, and even if he couldn't get news of his action into the papers, he would still refuse to be drafted "because it is something my conscience and my God have led me to."[12]

Most readers will recognize the influence of Jesus in Tom's reference to love. His comment on God and conscience seems to be a modern manifestation of God's activity among and within people as described by Jeremiah: "Behold the days are coming, says the Lord, when . . . I will put my law within them, and I will write it upon their hearts; and I will be their God, and they shall be my people" (Jer. 31:31–33). There is no other way to account for Tom's courage, considering the national feeling at that time toward draft resisters, a feeling mirrored in the judge's words as he sentenced Tom to five years in prison: "We must deal with you for the preservation of society."[13] To say that Tom was merely saving his own skin, that he was a coward, not only dismisses God from his action, but also dismisses the courage it takes to face the stigma of lack of patriotism and anticipated imprisonment.

As we know, thousands of other young men chose a similar path—or left the country. Although many of them have not had an opportunity to state their reasons in print, one suggestive substitute is a matter of public record. In 1971, poll-taker Louis Harris asked members of the younger generation, "Which book has most influenced your life?" One of the four favorites was John Griffin's *Black Like Me,* but the book receiving the largest number of votes was the Bible. Remember, this was not a poll of Jesus People, but of a cross section of the student mainstream.[14]

Students also presented dramatic witness to the Word live and in color in St. Cloud, Minnesota, in December 1968. Bishop George Speltz had just begun his Christmas Eve sermon when, with the aid of electronic equipment somewhere in the vicinity of the church, a more youthful voice was heard over the public address system. It asked:

George, why haven't you said anything about the war in Vietnam? Why haven't you said anything about whether it's right or wrong to kill another human being? Am I really supposed to believe the things I was taught in church such as "Thou shalt not kill" and "Love your neighbor as yourself" . . . or are you just putting me on?[15]

That some younger members of our society should turn their thoughts and words toward the Bible and the Church shows the kind of struggle in which they believed themselves engaged, and the One to whose Word they found themselves responding. Moreover, it suggests that while God may have written his law upon their hearts, he did not do so without a pen. Many adults, including parents, consigned draft-resisting to cowardice, which is the height of irony since what many of the young men were doing was merely taking seriously the teachings of their parents and churches. This was expressed with unmistakable clarity by a mother of a conscientious objector. She wrote:

We played a tremendous part in his decision before he ever began thinking really seriously about war and peace, because we have made great efforts to bring Denny and the rest of the children up in this philosophy of loving your fellow men. *But we ourselves have never extended our thinking into the larger issue of killing and the draft.* He extended it logically and arrived at his position, which is, "If I love, I don't kill." *We had just never gotten that far.*[16]

Most parents would readily agree that they did not raise their sons to be soldiers. Nevertheless the call to arms has often been heard in our land. That the call to love others, at home and abroad, should reach the inner ear points to a breakthrough of unprecedented proportions from somewhere. The flowers of justice, peace, and love that appeared in the young in the sixties may have grown from seeds planted by their progenitors, but it was the Eternal Incognito Parent who provided them with inspiration and dedication.

Parents exerted another influence on their campus brood during the sixties, one which few of them were probably aware of. While adults were making tanks, planes, and ships to contain communism (and to send their offspring to college), their children were being exposed in classroom communities to the beliefs and writings of Karl Marx and his associates. This exposure would probably have remained purely academic, had they not received confirmation of these teachings from their anti-Marxist parents.

For example, the student read in Marx's *Economic and Philosophical Manuscripts of 1844* that when a man labors as a human being he feels like an animal.[17] Immediately he remembered the groans of his hard-working father about it being a dog-eat-dog world. The world in which the parent spent much of his time was a jungle, which, as Marx put it, alienated man from himself.

"When I started here the place was like a family; now it's every man for himself," a Stanley Tool foreman in New Britain, Connecticut, told his son and daughter home for vacation; in their heads echoed Marx's thoughts about people being alienated from other people. Labor and management are both affected by this alienation, but, in *The Holy Family,* Marx wrote that whereas the possessing class is comfortable in it, the proletariat is annihilated by it.[18] To the student it was suddenly clear why Dad did not always look forward to getting up in the morning.

"You get the feeling," lamented an assembly line worker in Detroit, "that you're a machine." To his son this sounded like a repeat of what Marx had said more than one hundred years earlier about the laborer being a commodity, a piece of merchandise.[19] His labor is reduced to the point where the only thing he has to sell is himself. Man is human capital, a long number in a factory. As the folk song puts it, he "owes his soul to the company store." Thus, all over the United States, students discovered at home that what Marx had said about reality was the truth, even in the land of the middle class. They discovered that although what Marx stood for was labeled "communist" in the most derogatory tones, his concern was basically human. Parents, who denounced him and were hard at work to crush his twentieth-century impact, confirmed his diagnosis and unwittingly bore witness to its credibility. Finding definitive expression of parental thought in the man proclaimed Public Enemy Number One prompted many of the young to conclude that America's adults had condemned Marx and his cause without having read one line that he wrote.

One can understand the consternation of parents when their offspring came home from college and didn't seem to share their enthusiasm for the war. But, at the same time, given the similarity between the gut reactions of these parents and the thought of the nineteenth-century socialist, one can better understand the perplexity of the children: Why kill an enemy who sounds just like your father?

A NATION CONFRONTS THE ISSUES

Although it seemed for a while that the younger members of the family tree were out on a limb, it was not long before some older branches and even trunks made known their support. In retrospect, one can see how their backgrounds enhanced the impact of the truth upon the nation.

One of the first was a man with twelve million reasons to back the young, a man with a vested interest in the new generation, since he had helped foster it with his best-selling book on child care. When those whose childhood health he had nurtured were being conscripted for a premature demise, Dr. Benjamin Spock was unable to muffle his objection. The pressure of truth compelled him to follow the destiny of his huge family, even if it meant an end to his pediatric practice, reputation, and personal freedom. The issue, accentuated by his profession, was clear: Children were born to live, not die.

If the witness of Dr. Spock made some waves, that of two brother priests rocked the boat. First they entered a Selective Service office in Catonsville, Maryland, and, taking the draft records to the parking lot, set fire to them. A year later they entered the Washington, D.C., office of Dow Chemical and began throwing papers out the fourth floor window. Then blood was spilled on records, as a symbol of what napalm did to the bodies of Vietnamese villagers. Finished with this act of civil disobedience the priests and their companions sat down to wait for the police. The purpose of the Berrigan brothers was not sabotage; no windows were broken and the office was not damaged. The purpose was to get before the public an "Open Letter to the Corporations of America," which read in part:

We are outraged by the death-dealing exploitation of people . . . and of all the poor and powerless who are victimized by your profit-seeking ventures. In your mad pursuit of profit, you, and others like you, are causing the psychological and physical destruction of mankind. We urge all to join us as we say no to this madness.[20]

Herbert B. Doan, president of Dow Chemical, did not exactly share their position, but, ironically, his reply sent truth reverberating in the national psyche. "Any group that feels it has the right to destroy the property of others has quite clearly gone beyond the limit of legitimate dissent."[21] Without realizing it, he had put into words what we were doing in Vietnam. In denying one truth he unwittingly affirmed another.

The same sort of ironical repercussions surfaced elsewhere.

Fifteen hundred miles away, in St. Louis, three hundred parents added their own witness to the pressure of truth when they requested the removal of Sister Joann Malone, a teacher in their high school, who had participated in the Dow raid. To these parents her actions had been criminal. Moreover, they were out of character; she should have kept her religion in the classroom where she taught it. When the people of St. Cloud, Minnesota, had had the thought of Vietnam intrude upon their Christmas sermon, they were outraged because the church was no place into which to bring the world (neither was it proper to address a bishop by his Christian name). The parents in St. Louis had the opposite reaction: The world was no place to bring the church. At the time, at least, they did not realize that Sister Joann *was* teaching religion by her witness.

For many in the pulpit, too, this kind of truth was like being hit with a pew. Realization came abruptly for some, slowly for others, but eventually numerous church leaders and laymen were made aware how far religion had moved from reality, from the social, economic, and political arenas, where gut issues are decided. Truth, like penetrating oil, began to seep into the naves and chancels of America. Faith was not alive where we lived; the words *peace* and *love* and *God* had come up empty.

Further west in California, an associate professor of philosophy at UCLA sat in jail awaiting trial for murder and kidnapping. She had belonged to the Birmingham, Alabama, church where four girls had been killed by a bomb in 1963, victims of the fight for racial justice. Now she was an atheist. Yet, during the sixteen months that Angela Davis languished in jail without bond, she became the Joan of Arc of political prisoners in America. Several factors merged to create a charismatic effect on many people, especially students. Her skin pigment blended in with a decade of concern for civil rights. Her sex bolstered the sentiment for women's equality that was gaining momentum at the time. However, it was her self-avowed Marxist politics that quietly but devastatingly communicated a word of truth to the nation. That the government would keep her in punitive detention while awaiting trial and, at the same time, entertain foreign communist visitors at the White House with charm and congeniality, scored the administration with incredible duplicity. When she finally did come up for trial in 1972, she was acquitted.

The courtroom is the place where the truth, the whole truth, and nothing but the truth is supposed to resound, and during the sixties it did, but not always as one might have expected. Take, for example, the judge who put Tom Rodd in prison "for the preservation of society." Then consider the trial of Dr. Spock. He and those tried with him for conspiring to give advice to draft resisters welcomed the trial as an opportunity to bring the morality and legality of the war before the public. The judge never gave them the chance; instead he unwittingly did it himself, first by not allowing the reasons for the action of the defendants to be presented as evidence, and then by lecturing the jury for fifty minutes on bringing in a verdict of guilty.[22] Unintentionally, the judge informed the nation, by way of the press, that the government's case, and the war, were indeed on shaky ground. A year later his fear was substantiated when a higher court cleared the doctor of the charge.

In the Berrigan trial the defendants were allowed to speak their witness in court. The priests asserted that the lives of young Americans were the property of God, not the government, and that no one could deny that compared to the draftees, the draft records were but pieces of paper. With outright sympathy, the judge, near the conclusion of the trial, joined the defendants in praying the "Our Father." However, despite sympathies with the accused, he had to instruct the jury not to "judge this case on the basis of conscience."[23] When courtroom officials will not or cannot allow the conscience of a defendant to be considered by a jury of his peers, then the jails become shrines.

In California, on the other hand, a mother tried to meet the government on its own level of technicality by refusing to grant permission for her son to register for the draft on the grounds that he was only eighteen. Without permission, she observed, a minor could not get married, could not own property, and, in 1969, could not vote. Moreover, being legally responsible for her son, she could not place him in the position of doing something counter to the beliefs by which he had been taught to live (she had not raised him to be a soldier). The judge would not listen to reason, and the son, sharing his mothers convictions, went to prison to serve a four-year sentence. His two brothers were soon to follow. But in this case, as in those like it, the government only succeeded in illustrating that "when the law treats a reasonable conscientious act as a crime, it subverts its own power. It invites civil disobedience. It impairs the very habits which nourish and preserve the law."[24]

Perhaps the strongest indictment the administration rendered against itself during its struggle with war dissenters came when Daniel Ellsberg was brought to trial for making public the Pentagon's own analysis of the war situation. This analysis frankly acknowledged on page after page our errors in Vietnam. Here was the bureaucratic home of the Armed Forces admitting that the war was a mistake, not in morality but in execution, and the government, as if to tell the world that it was dedicated to the suppression of the truth, proceeded to bring Ellsberg to court for his disclosure. The trial never went to the jury; the case was dismissed.

Of all the confrontations with truth to which the nation was exposed during the struggle against U.S. presence in Vietnam, none transmitted more pressure than that of the veterans who returned to protest their own war. Many citizens found it possible to deny the protest of students, clergy, and doctors, but the sight of legless or armless veterans moving in a wheel chair parade was difficult to refute. They had the scars of Vietnam futility carved on their bodies. And when they so described it, truth came home to roost. The presence of 350,000 students in Washington could be dismissed as cowardice or unpatriotic fervor, but the sight of decorated veterans throwing their Purple Hearts and Medals of Honor on the Capitol veranda was something else. It was enough to make the most war-oriented members of Congress tremble for awhile.[25]

Many parents had wanted to believe that military service would turn their boys into men. My Lai informed the nation that it didn't always happen. Some did return as mature, responsible human beings, but not as their parents had anticipated. "We are ashamed of what we did," the leader of one veterans' group confessed. [26] Citizens were brought face to face with the fact that no matter how dead the enemy might be, the consciences of those who had killed him were quite alive. Because of the strength of student sentiment, the climate at home finally made it possible for returning veterans to ventilate their feelings of anger, bitterness, and guilt, knowing that somebody would listen. In previous wars young men returning from the trenches of Verdun or the islands of the Pacific had immediately sensed the pride of the home team and kept their thoughts to themselves; Indochina ended this illusion. This time, instead of bottling it up in the American Legion and V.F.W. halls, they could let it all hang out. This time, therapy was received in public, not just in the privacy of the psychiatrist's office.[27]

THE RESULTS OF TRUTH

One of the results of the United States' confrontation with truth during the sixties and early seventies was a cessation of the bombing and of the presence of active American troops in Vietnam. Several facets of truth combined to bring this about; not least was the unwillingness of so many soldiers to continue the war. With the pursuit of peace undercutting the will to kill the designated enemy, there was no choice; the troops had to be brought home.

Another factor was the election of 1972. Four years before, Richard Nixon had won the presidency on a promise to end the war, so its continuation raised questions as to his credibility. In addition to his 1968 promise there were the statements he had made to the protesting students: "I'm a devout Quaker. I'm against killing as much as you are and I want to bring the boys home."[28] Because it was an election year, he had to show that he was a man of his word.

There were also rumblings along the Russian-Chinese border. The time was ripe for the United States to gain their separate confidences, and the president knew that doing so would put pressure on Hanoi to negotiate.

The key factor, however, was the direct influence exerted by the peace movement on the mood of the nation. Nixon's visits to Peking and Moscow were bold strokes, but they could never have occurred if the nation had been completely behind the war. A

nation of hawks would never have tolerated its leader turning
dove, even if he was a Quaker. The visits would not have been
made if Nixon had thought they would spell political suicide.

I do not deny that Nixon took advantage of an opportunity. I
affirm, however, that the existence of a vocal minority, beseech-
ing him to give peace a chance, served as a mirror for his declara-
tions and aspirations. Having declared himself for peace, he
knew he was forced either to live up to his verbal commitment one
way or another, or to lose the election and go down in history as
the kind of person the academic community had assessed him to
be. The same ego that had made it of historic importance for
Richard Nixon not to lose the war now made it of historic importance for him to win the peace.

COMING TO TERMS WITH INTEGRITY

A second result of God's political activity was the passion for
integrity that surfaced in 1973 and 1974 seemingly in response to
the Watergate affair. Actually, it was the result of a decade of
resisting the truth from Vietnam, resistance reflected in the attitude toward students. At first the reaction to students appeared
irrational, such as people feeling in 1970 that campus unrest was
the greatest problem facing the nation, surpassing the war, the
cost of living, and drug addiction.[29] Although campus unrest in
many schools amounted to a handful of students sitting on the
floor of a building, it produced a cry for law and order, while
three hundred tons of bombs dropped in Indochina each day
produced no such cry. Vietnam made campus violence seem like
child's play, which it was. Yet, students at Kent State could be
indicted for throwing stones while National Guardsmen firing
bullets, and killing several students, were exonerated.

Actually, the country's reaction to the student population,
while tragic, was understandable. It was like that of the king who
had the messenger beheaded for bringing him bad news. We
were indeed getting the message. The very fact of resisting it was
a way of affirming its veracity, for we do not get upset over what
does not reach us. It could not yet be acknowledged in public, but
in the privacy of the mind, where the Spirit "speaks," it was very

much at work. We knew, albeit unconsciously, that it was leading to a revision of priorities and values. Consequently, when knowledge of Watergate opened up, it was as if someone had pulled his finger from a dike. It began as a tiny drip, but soon, very soon, it was the whole sea. Employing a well-known biblical metaphor, with the unassimilated log in our own eyes pointing the way, we could see clearly the splinter in the Nixon administration. When he resigned, therefore, the nation breathed a sigh of relief. However, the word "pardon" brought back the past with a vengeance. Pardoning Nixon for Watergate was not the real problem; pardoning him for Vietnam was the emotional issue, for we had not yet forgiven ourselves for that. Watergate had been but a surrogate all along. This is also why in one breath we could admit that it had been wrong to send troops to Vietnam, but say in the next that those who were the first to tell us about the wrong must work their way back into our good graces. The truth was very much alive, though repressed. It was at work though we did not understand it at that time.

The peak (or depth) of our sublimation was reached during the 1974 congressional election, when righteousness in public office became the campaign issue and every candidate publicized his income and his integrity, as if the two were synonymous. Washington was described as the birthplace of a spiritual renaissance, where Bible study and prayer groups were proliferating. *Time* sensationalized it as usual by referring to the "God network" in the nation's capital.[30] How much is truly of God and how much is of man will become known when these pious legislators confront defense spending, world hunger, and bussing. Our response as individuals and as a nation to the Third World at home and abroad will for years to come be the territory on which righteousness will be tested.

BY THEIR STRIPES

One further result of the pressure of truth deserves to be mentioned. It is fortunate that there were those people in the United States and overseas who were willing to rock the boat, for the course on which the ship of state was embarked, and still is in

some quarters, was making a prophet out of John Quincy Adams.
On July 4, 1821, he said in an address:

Whenever the standard of freedom and independence has been or shall
be unfurled, there will be America's heart. But she goes not abroad in
search of monsters to destroy. . . . If she did the fundamental maxims of
her policy would insensibly change from liberty to force. She would no
longer be the ruler of her own spirit.[31]

Thanks to the vision and courage of the young in response to
the political activity of God, we have changed course, somewhat.
Indeed, they were the real patriots during the years of protest.
And in this contest it is interesting to note that here history was
only repeating itself. When the thirteen colonies were on the
brink of revolution, more than two hundred years ago, many
solid citizens frowned on patriotism as a sin against the Crown.
Those loyal to established British rule were called Tories; those
who dissented from it were labeled Patriots. More recently the
labels and their meanings were changed so that those who de-
fended the establishment were the "patriots" and those who chal-
lenged it were called radicals, rebels, or effete snobs.

In biblical parlance, however, these radicals were suffering
servants. As Isaiah said, the "suffering servant" grew up before
the people "like a root out of dry ground." No one expected the
new generation to hold or apply the ideals they have shown.
Dressed in jeans and wearing their hair long, they had "no form
or comeliness, . . . no beauty that we should desire. . . . " Therefore, we rejected them. They became children "of sorrows and
acquainted with grief." Both at home and away they died in our
place. Yet, the chastisement of our peace was upon them, and by
their stripes have many of us been healed, though not all (Isa.
53:1–5). There is more than symbolism in their appearance, their
vision, and in their convictions. There is an affinity, an identity
even, with the one who walked the dusty roads of Palestine
centuries ago in sandals and God's name, speaking of peace,
justice, and liberty for humankind, and taking the consequences
upon himself. What we have witnessed is the participation of the
Prince of Peace in the historical process for the furtherance of
God's kingdom here on earth.

This did not bestow upon them an indelible character. Even militant youth have been forced to bring their methods more in harmony with their goals so as not to be counter-productive. "No generation is free from inner resentment and extreme reactions. Each generation will have to learn to look at itself with the same sincerity it demands of the other."[32] However, God is at work, and ultimately no one escapes the means and the ends to which he is dedicated.

A cynic might say that the election year was good for something, but to a person of faith the conflict in Vietnam was good for something. No one need feel that his son died there in vain, or that the reaction of his son or daughter here at home was disloyal or unpatriotic. All of them helped arouse within us a disdain for war as a means of settling anything, and a desire for the light from Fort Jesus that we shall consider in a later chapter. Moreover, to its very end in 1975, the war in Indochina was a confrontation with truth, one for which America could say, "Thanks, I needed that." The advertizing world sees to it that illusion is the air we breathe, and we cannot blame national leaders entirely for lying us into Vietnam and Cambodia and then trying to lie us out. We had come to accept the lie as normal. We had come to accept only what we wanted to hear. But history has done us a favor. We know both sides now, and though sadder, many are at least a trifle wiser. Many now know that truth cannot ultimately be denied, even here on earth. There are those who still prefer not to look at the horror of our part in the war, or who cannot bear it, but we would be so bold as to suggest that few of us would greet another Vietnam with enthusiasm. Indeed, Vietnam will one day be but a memory, but we can hope that what it has done to shape the means and the ends of the superpowers, as well as those of private citizens, will not fade away.

ISSUES FOR DISCUSSION

1. The pressure of truth is no more than a psychological phenomenon.

2. The reactions of many students revealed a strong ethical-theistic base.

3. What Karl Marx stood for was labeled "communist," but his concern was essentially human.

4. The Berrigan brothers were working within the system.

5. Through anti-war veterans the truth of Vietnam came home to roost.

6. The visits to Peking and Moscow would not have been made had we as a nation been 100 percent behind the war.

7. Dr. Spock had no reason to protest the war.

8. Adult response to students was like the king who had a messenger beheaded for bringing him bad news.

9. We owe the students of America a debt of gratitude for their stand on the Indochina War.

NOTES

1. Matthew 24:34. With the kingdom would come a state of peace, but how God would accomplish this was left unsaid.

2. Paul's main concern here is to obey the law and not rock the boat—maintain the status quo.

3. David Manning White, *People, Society, and Mass Communications* (New York: The Free Press, 1964), pp. 164–65.

4. In Prague, Russian soldiers were bombarded with questions. Obviously embarrassed, they stared blankly into the distance. Many didn't know why they were there and were apologetic. "We are only following orders," a young paratrooper said. "The political decisions are not our affair" (*Time,* August 30, 1968), p. 23.

5. *New York Times,* May 16, 1967, p. 9.

6. J. William Fulbright, *The Arrogance of Power* (New York: Vintage Books, 1966), p. 16.

7. On a memorial plaque at Concord Bridge are recorded these words:
They came 3,000 miles alive
to keep the past upon its throne.
Unheard beyond the ocean tide
their English mother made them moan.

8. This was shared with the author by a returned veteran, whose home is in Brockton, Mass.

9. Bud Collins, *Boston Globe,* February 16, 1968.

10. The Alice whose restaurant inspired the song's title is still serving food in Stockbridge, though at a different location. The place is a kind of shrine for young adults who visit the community and remember. In awe they stand and wait for their order to be filled by Alice and her crew.

11. This young man's self-immolation took place a few weeks after he had received his draft notice; it was reported by the Associated Press, May 12, 1970. The first American to have done this was Norman Morrison, who set fire to himself in November 1965 outside the Pentagon.

12. Quoted by Gene Stanford, ed., *Generation Rap* (New York: Dell, 1971), pp. 19, 21, 22.

13. *Ibid.,* p. 24 (Court Record, August 18, 1964). Federal Court, Pittsburgh.

14. *Life,* January 8, 1971, p. 30.

15. *National Catholic Reporter,* January 1, 1969, p. 5. This did not appear in most daily newspapers.

16. *Ibid.,* January 8, 1969, p. 2.

17. Karl Marx, *Economic and Philosophical Manuscripts of 1844,* trans. Martin Milligan (New York: International Publishers, 1964), p. 111.

18. Quoted by Alasdair MacIntyre in *Marxism and Christianity* (New York, Schocken Books, 1968), p. 58.

19. Karl Marx and Friedrich Engels, *The Communist Manifesto,* trans. Samuel Moore (New York: Washington Square Press, 1971), p. 68.

20. *National Catholic Reporter,* April 2, 1969.

21. *Ibid.*

22. *Boston Globe,* June 15, 1968.

23. Walter Kerr, "The Trial of the Catonsville Nine," *New York Times,* February 14, 1971.

24. Judge Charles Wyzanski, Jr., in the case of John Sisson, Jr., a nonreligious conscientious objector, *New York Times,* April 2, 1969, p. 2.

25. As soon as a minority of the marching students threatened traffic, the elected officials who had professed to be won over by the veterans said the students had spoiled it.

26. Cutting off ears and hooking wires to genitals were described. Helicopter pilots told of maneuvering planes so as to strike the heads of peasant farmers with the ship's skids. (See Seymour M. Hersh, "The Decline and Near Fall of the U.S. Army," *Saturday Review,* December 1972, p. 58.)

27. On Labor Day evening, September 4, 1972, a Vietnam vet called the Jerry Williams talk show on WBZ radio in Boston and told how he would go into villages after napalm was dropped and find human beings fused together like pieces of metal that has been soldered. "When you're over there you condone it," he said. "It's when you get home that it bothers you." (The full text of this call appeared in *The Boston Globe,* October 13, 1972, p. 24.)

28. These words were uttered on May 9, 1970 at the Lincoln Memorial by Nixon when he spoke to some students he encountered there during a walk. See *New York Times,* May 10, 1970.

29. These were the results of a Gallup Poll taken in May 1970.

30. *Time,* August 26, 1974, p. 70.

31. See Adams Papers Microfilm no. 452. Quoted by Edward H. Tatum, Jr., in *The United States and Europe, 1815–1823: A Study in the Background of the Monroe Doctrine* (New York, 1967), p. 244.

32. Lewis S. Feuer, "Conflict of Generations," *Saturday Review,* January 18, 1969, p. 69.

CHAPTER 6

God's Economic Activity

The flow of goods and services may seem like a strictly human activity. However, as published in God's word, when it comes to the evenness of this flow, God has expressed a decided interest. Although the felt need for economic justice on a worldwide scale is an indication of this interest, the experience of one country in particular is noteworthy, in part because the official policy there is a nontheistic one, and in part because in giving top priority to economic justice it has captured the attention and imagination of the world. In a report on his recent return to China, a former missionary said: "The entrance of new China into active participation in the world community may well be the most important single event in the history of the twentieth century."[1]

Since most of us have not been to China to see for ourselves what is happening there, we are dependent upon the eyewitness accounts of those who have. And upon reading the articles that have appeared in periodicals and newspapers since the door to China opened in 1972, the impression one receives from those who visit there is that something bordering on the miraculous has taken place. It matters not whether the visitor's background be that of a journalist, educator, athlete, actress, politician, doctor, sociologist, former missionary, man or woman, few can hide their enthusiasm.[2]

This enthusiasm is itself surprising. With years of hostility toward China as part of our official policy, it is to be expected that American visitors would bring with them a suitcase full of unfavorable biases. One writer acknowledged that Western visitors bring suspicion with them but that most of them become convinced that what they see is authentic and not staged.[3]

In this chapter we will discuss the credibility of this eyewitness enthusiasm, why even the skeptical visitor finds it difficult to hide his esteem. What disarms him, or wins him over from a preconceived opinion?

In assessing the enthusiasm of visitors to China, I would first call attention to the spirit of the Chinese people. It is contagious. Pride in their accomplishments and confidence in their future are discernible immediately, and when people meet eyeball to eyeball, the inner spirit usually comes through. A good actor could fake it, but training 700 million people to be good actors would be harder than making the kind of changes that could prompt authentic expressions of such feeling.

Visitors to China repeatedly hear such phrases as "before liberation" and "after liberation," the way early Christians are reputed to have spoken of life before and after Christ. The change for the Chinese took place October 1, 1949, when liberation from foreign domination, landlordism, and tyranny was achieved. In one village school a series of drawings by teachers and children tells the history of one of the village families before liberation, and through this, of the village itself. "It was work for the landlords, no bed at night, sell your daughter, live as beggars."[4] In the same school there was a glass case in which stood a beggar's bowl, a landlord's false-bottomed measuring basket, and the wooden pillow one family used for eighty years.

Viewing the present China against its past, it is not hard to see why the people's spirit is exuberant. Bicycles greatly outnumber cars, and there are few television sets, but the necessities of life—food, clothing, and shelter—are present in ample proportions. People are healthy and all who are able work; there are no beggars in the streets, no signs of prostitution. One reporter with the Nixon entourage, who had lived in China before 1949, made it a point to break away without escort to mix with people in parks, shops, and on side streets.[5] He found them better fed and better dressed than before. Housing was much improved though far below U.S. standards, and back alleys, previously littered with junk, were as clean as front walks.

"Food is very inexpensive," volunteered Senator Hugh Scott. "They eat far better than the Russians ... and they eat with imagination and variety."[6] Syndicated columnist Joseph Alsop bore witness to this when he wrote how popular restaurant eating is in Peking. Not only were many places available, but they were jammed with working people, lacking the smallest outward pretensions.[7] Presumably, if in the past one's stomach was shrinking from famine or malnutrition, a full stomach of plain food is like filet mignon in Benihana's of Tokyo.

One further way of accounting for this spirit is that improvements for the people are the products of the people. Rather than depend on outside help, the Chinese have done it for themselves. Mao Tse-tung had the vision to see that there was latent power in the people that could be released in sufficient quantity and quality to overcome mountains of poverty, ignorance, and psychological defeat. Mao demonstrated this faith in no uncertain terms, and the people in turn responded. Instead of inviting in foreign advisors and foreign capital to assure a rapid centralized economic growth, he chose the slower way of encouraging development regionally and locally down into the communes and within them in the production teams. This led to a release of creative energy and a sense of participation in decision making that surely contributes to the contagious spirit that spreads to most visitors.

LOSING THE LUGGAGE

One reason the suspicion visitors lug with them to China soon gives way to enthusiasm is the degree to which their hosts are open and honest about China's failings. Indeed, the Chinese are the first to point out that their society is far from perfect. They have made great strides, but there is still a long way to go. Progress has been made toward a classless society that would have exceeded Marx's fondest expectations, but the preferred status of persons in certain positions persists, along with male chauvinism. With winsome candor, factory workers told of the period of tension that prevailed when lathe operators and draftsmen had to get acquainted with each other and each other's job as a result of the Cultural Revolution of 1966. At first the relations were "terrible," one man told a visitor. "Slowly we learned from each other."[8] A professor in anthropology sent to work in the villages during the Revolution related how difficult it was at first, "but the people were patient. Now," he said, "I know a bit about physical work . . . and I can hardly look at my past writing on peasants. Now I see them not as subjects to be studied, but as laboring comrades."[9]

If one wanted to be cynical, of course, one could say that the Chinese were quite aware of the value of honesty, and used it to score points. This would indeed take the edge off it, but the part that openness and honesty has long played in their culture puts the edge back on. On a framed poster in Peking's Forbidden City were the words "Be Open and Above board." They were written 500 years ago during the Ming dynasty.[10] Such background would allow one to observe that the ideas of atheistic communism did not destroy Chinese moral integrity, but found it to be quite compatible.

The Chinese are aware of visitors wanting to move about on their own. They know the hidden message that guided tours can convey. In fact they have an analogy for it. They liken it to "viewing flowers on horseback." Although there are sights they do not want visitors to miss, they are open to guests dismounting for a closer look. In 1974, eleven students from East Coast universities visited China for three and one-half weeks; they reported that they were allowed to "wander wherever they wanted to, subject only to curious stares from passersby and occasional crowds of friendly children."[11] The message this conveyed was that the Chinese have nothing to hide.

The Chinese, having observed that evil shuns light, have turned this truth into a way of purging society of corruption. People are encouraged to expose alleged corruption in government officials, the way the press does in the United States. Party leaders who pocket wages that belong to the people or police who wrongfully detain or mistreat someone soon find their names and faces on posters publicizing their crimes. It serves as a deterrent.

Another reason for the zeal of American visitors is the manner in which stereotypes of life behind the Bamboo Curtain soon become excess baggage, unnecessary to carry around. For example, when Martin and Johnson observed that people were relaxed,[12] it would seem reasonable to assume that they expected them to be otherwise, an otherwise that points to the image of Big Brother listening in on conversations through hidden microphones, making everyone nervous. When Scott remarked how the people are happy, it would be safe to infer that he went to China expecting to find them dejected and morose, especially when he notes, "We had been told that the Chinese are very serious, but it's far from the truth."[13]

The same process of reasoning can be pursued in response to observations and questions about family life in China. When the interviewer of Senator Mansfield asked, "Have traditional family ties broken down?" he had for some reason assumed that they had or might have.[14] That reason is the image lurking in the shadows of children being sent off by the state to state-owned facilities at an early age. By the same token, the missionary's observation that many small families were on picnics in the gardens of the Summer Palace causes one to wonder why such a common, normal occurence would interest him.[15] He was either surprised to find this going on, or assumed readers in America might be. Also, the comments of writers about people being paid for their work implies a preconceived impression to the contrary. Visitors to noncommunist countries would take this for granted. The need for incentive is recognized by the Chinese. Rubbish collectors, for example, will work up to 7:00 P.M. because they are paid so much per barrel as an inducement for a menial task. And such income can even be used to purchase private property, a reality that goes totally against the impression we have of a Marxist state. All of these discoveries would tend to make visitors from America feel at home; the Chinese are not such bad guys after all, not at all like what we had been led to think.

THE GREENING OF CHINA

Although stereotypes gained over the years may have sharpened the sensitivities of visitors exposed to their truth or falsehood, perhaps the greatest source of enthusiasm for what is happening in China is the state of the union here at home. According to a Harris poll of December 1973, seventy-five percent of the inhabitants of the United States believe that there is something "deeply wrong" with our nation because the rich seem to be getting richer and the poor poorer. However, even if a person stressed only what was right about America, he or she would have to be extremely insensitive to totally ward off the maturing awareness of the majority. Even an unconscious pickup of these vibrations would be enough to make visitors to China receptive to a society where the needs to which our difficulties point are being so effectively met.

One reason for the above awareness is the high visibility of the economic caste system in America. One writer has presented a literal explication of this assertion. The thesis of James Hamilton's *The Thunder of Bare Feet* is that in countries and communities where there are hills, the wealthy inevitably live on them, unwittingly communicating to the population a high-low class message.[16] Presumably even geography has its psychology.

Expressways also contribute to this awareness. People by the thousands, from hills and level areas, horsepower their way into the city from the suburbs without dismounting. They return at five o'clock, leaving low-income folks behind with the daily reminder that they are second-class citizens.

Television has also played its part. Watching sex and violence provides a temporary escape for the occupant of an inner city tenement, until the time for commercials. Since these are, of economic necessity, pitches to the affluent (middle class included), the poor are perpetually exposed to what they are missing. After years of this the tension is coming to a head in the form of hostility and crime.

The educational system in America at the secondary level feeds this economic structure. With ample funds youth can go to prep schools where small classes provide individual attention from teachers. The majority, bound for college or a job requiring a general education, attend public high schools, while those with a proficiency for the trades can enter state-operated technical schools, third from the top in the trinity of educational opportunities. Unlike the faces of God, the three remain separate and unequal, in image if not in fact.

Unquestionably aware of their own caste system, American visitors to China cannot help but be impressed with the educational activity there. All students, through the graduate level, perform at least two hours of physical labor a day; they also use their long vacations to go to the country and work with the villagers. Moreover, before 1967 only the elite went to college. Now the student body of any school is composed of children from peasant and laboring families, as well as from the professions.

We graduate people with degrees and titles and the rights and privileges which thereto appertain are accustomed to income, prestige, and degrees of luxury. The seeds of our caste system were brought to America from Europe, but the harvest now includes greed and anger. Professional people, such as doctors and lawyers (there are exceptions), feel entitled to exorbitant fees, thereby prompting victims who can afford it to sue in cases of malpractice, but building in all a layer of anger that waits to be exploited for good or ill. As long as this continues, the direction of the United States is downhill. The thunder of bare feet will in time grow louder. Deep down most Americans know this, and this is why China looks good to visitors from our side of the ocean.

As noted earlier, visitors to China have been told how the preferred status of some people persists. What they see everywhere, however, is the way the Cultural Revolution helped the masses. Party leaders used to eat in restaurants without the slightest notion of how things looked in the kitchen. Since 1966 they have learned how to cook. Top government officials travel by bicycle, just as the rest of the people do. Doctors are no longer addressed by professional titles; they are simply referred to as health workers. Gone, too, is the pompous medical air that so often accompanies titles and makes people wilt and smolder. In Sha Shr Yu, an isolated commune in northeast China, the health worker is a young woman of twenty-six, the daughter of a bourgeois family from the industrial city of Tang-shan.[17] Half her days she works in the fields with the people, and it is this that has moved villagers to accept her advice on birth control and ways to improve sanitation. At first she was frightened at leaving her native city, but her work in the fields soon created a rapport with people, and the fear departed. The Chinese have put the "serve" back into service.

If a visitor from America has difficulty seeing the state of the union at home, there is a good chance that China will sharpen his vision. This is especially true with regard to the part competition and cooperation play in the two countries. The United States prides itself on free enterprise economics. What is coming through to us now, however, is that few people are free. Free enterprise depends upon competition, but for there to be genuine competition, a handicap system, a reality long recognized in such sports as bowling and golf, must be in force to keep the sides relatively even and offset the natural power of some over others. Ironically, what Americans know at an existential level is that those who are most bullish on free enterprise are those who are unwittingly destroying it, or keeping it from really working. Doing their utmost to obtain a corner on the market, to eliminate the competition, they, in effect, render the system null and void. Their attitude produces huge chain supermarkets and corporations—and small corner stores that have to keep open seven days a week to stay in business. Minus strong government control, those with the money, opportunity, talent, and the right color rise. Others fall. In a society where it's every man for himself, only the fittest survive.

Two people, speaking in quite separate contexts, recently gave good examples of the growing awareness of this dawning. In an article describing Chicago's Board of Trade, where nearly all our country's foodstuffs are bought and sold, one independent member said, "For me it was good financially, but for everyone who makes money here, somebody loses. Three out of four speculators lose money and there's bound to be one big winner."[18] Political scientist Charles Lindblom of Yale asserts that capitalism depends on women and blacks accepting a second class economic role so that high income can reward the initiative of other persons. How much equality capitalism can tolerate is a key question.[19]

China, by contrast, has stimulated incentive by placing cooperation and mutual encouragement above competition and rugged individualism, and priorities, be they good or bad, always produce results. One visitor, for example, observed how workers no longer sit around discussing salaries and complaining, but instead, share ideas on how to cut overhead expenses and how to do better. Before, when someone found a more efficient way of doing something, he kept it to himself in order to produce more than his fellows, and thus earn more. Now, when someone discovers a better method, he immediately offers it to the group, since the only way he can benefit from it is if all benefit from it. Because both profits and decisions are shared, everyone has a sense of responsibility for the outcome. Work has become a transforming force.[20]

The visitor who told about the rapport in the tool and die shop noted that prior to 1967 blueprints were drawn upstairs; and if they did not work, the lathe workers downstairs were blamed for it. Because of the new relationship, fewer mistakes are made, the work goes faster, and the bad feelings are gone.[21] It could be added that these feelings were probably there all along, but suppressed. Now it is a new day in the factory, and the high morale in labor relations is obvious.

The difference between competition and cooperation is also apparent in the schools. In the United States grades and academic or athletic performance are what counts. Those who succeed do not complain, and those who fail frequently fall away. Efforts to reorient the purpose of education are exceedingly slow. In China visitors could not help but notice how the academic record is not what counts for advancement into positions of responsibility. What matters is a student's citizenship record—his demonstrated unselfishness, cooperativeness, good attitude toward physical labor, and enthusiasm for political activity.[22] Students and teachers devise examinations together, and students are expected to consult with each other on answers. In two of the four schools Mirsky visited, even the teachers took the tests. Never once did he hear a teacher tell a student, "That's wrong!" The usual response to a mistake was "Who can help this comrade?" (Although we may feel the word "comrade" is now tainted, it is in our dictionary, and the Chinese have proceeded to activate its meaning.) At a small nursery school, a very young child was struggling to lift a large toy block. After watching him for a moment, someone in the visiting group remarked that the block looked far too heavy for someone so small to lift all alone. The teacher smiled, nodded, and replied: "Exactly!"[23]

What Americans are seeing and believing at another level is the difference between a country that has a unifying purpose and one that has misplaced its purpose, or has a divisive one. In the latter case, the Russian people feel they are being denied the better things of life because of the Kremlin war machine. The Chinese, on the other hand, care for each other. "We believe," Senator Scott was told, "that we owe it to our people to see that they are adequately dressed, that food is plentiful, and that everybody shares it equally."[24] Until then, luxuries are taboo. This even holds true for minority groups who occupy fifty percent of the land area and constitute ten percent of the population. China is working hard at bringing the cultural riches of these groups into the whole stream of Chinese life.[25] Equal opportunities for education, work, and citizenship are open to everyone.

Visitors from America did not bring with them a similar sense. America does have a national purpose—liberty and justice for all. Unfortunately, capitalism, in its laissez-faire form, lacks the capacity to elicit a sense of mutual responsibility for its implementation, or to unite a nation. "Why are you so entranced by the Chinese?" Kissinger was asked in 1973. "Because," the ex-professor replied, "they have a Weltanschauung. The rest of us have lost our way."[26] Actually, however, what Kissinger and Nixon did by their visits to China was to make it possible for the rest of the world to receive a vision of what a society can be when its leadership is dedicated to lifting *all* its citizens from the depths of impoverishment.

In assessing the enthusiasm of Americans who visit China, we have not only indicated their credibility, but that of their Oriental hosts as well. We would not deny that the latter were aware of what is happening in America, or that the inherent weaknesses of capitalism have provided them with a kind of incentive for a different socio-economic approach to living. However, after twenty years of being closed for remodeling, China did not have to pay its people to smile for visitors. It was not necessary to distribute opium to the masses to give them a sense of euphoria. Their house was in order; it spoke for itself. Their very ability to be honest about their own weaknesses bore indirect witness to an inner security that could stem only from an overwhelming measure of success. What Americans experience and write about is the difference between the two nations, and the results of the different priorities to which each is dedicated. The grass always looks greener on the other side of the fence, but if one crosses the fence and discovers that it is greener, it is difficult to avoid a pleasant report.

MOVING MOUNTAINS

There is one other reason for the enthusiasm of visitors to China. Included in the mental luggage visitors from the West bring with them is the Bible. We in the West have been exposed to the tenets of Judeo-Christianity for centuries, and though capitalism is supreme during the week, the Word has served to give us a nodding acquaintance with the truth of God on Sunday morning. China is attractive because it is implementing the meaning embedded in the words we hear on weekends. How many of the visitors are aware of this we do not know. We do know some are. Yet, aware of it or not, we cannot deny that the biblical perspective that influenced the youthful thinking of Karl Marx has also made an impression upon us even though we have not been able economically to structure our society accordingly.

We can see this emerging in the way some visitors speak of Mao Tse-tung, whose picture, along with that of Marx, is everywhere. One might place more importance on the presence of his sayings on the walls of communes,[27] but of even greater import is the way the people relate to him. So impressed was Senator Mansfield with the reverence people have for Mao that he was moved to use New Testament terminology to describe it. "They heed his sayings as if they were part of the gospel," was the way he put it.[28] While aware that he was in the land of Confucius, Senator Scott also dipped into his religious heritage when he likened Maoism to a "theology of the Supreme Teacher."[29] For missionary Johnson it was the Old Testament that provided the analogy. He referred to Mao as the "Moses of Chinese liberation."[30] Moreover, just as the Hebrew people remember the pharaoh, and the freedom Moses obtained for them, so "one may expect Mao will be remembered and revered for many generations."

On the surface this looks and sounds like idolatry, and having espoused atheism, it does appear that he put himself in the place of the gods. What China has, however, is a man very much aware of the people's need for a leader, but who drew upon sources beyond himself for insight and inspiration. For example, there is the story of the Foolish Old Man of North Mountain, an oriental legend that Mao used in 1945 to inspire people with determination and persistence. A foolish old man and his sons were working to level two high mountains that stood in front of their home, removing one shovelful at a time. When a reputed wise old man came by and ridiculed the effort, the foolish one replied, unabashed, that after him and his sons, his grandsons and great-grandsons would continue with the task, and eventually the two mountains would be removed. They could not get any larger, and with each shovelful they would get that much smaller. According to the legend, God was moved by his faith, and he sent two angels who carried the mountains away on their backs (without crushing their wings). To Mao, the mountains that needed moving were those of imperialism and landlordism, and the god that he saw doing it was the Chinese people.

The story inspired the people with an abiding initiative. However, by its very use it cannot be said that the people did it themselves (the keynote of Mao's teaching). Mao's use of this story has inspired them with a faith, a faith that moves mountains.

It might at first seem that they have responded to two old men, one in a fable form, the other in the flesh, causing charisma to become incarnate among them and within them. However, there is more to this than two men. Isaiah was the first person to use a mountain to describe the injustice being perpetrated in a nation,[31] and it could very well be that Jesus had this in mind when he spoke of faith moving a mountain (Matt. 17:20). In any event, there is a point of identity here, and it is not in the topographical affinity, nor in metaphors being made out of mountains. It's not even basically in the use to which the metaphors are put. Basically, the point of identity is the Creator of all whose activity Isaiah was defining. What is coming through is a common Source of inspiration.

Whatever one calls Mao's economic thought, it cannot be written off as secular or pagan. Even atheist is no longer accurate. Mao did at one time deport missionaries, but in importing the ideas of Marx, he unwittingly introduced the people of China to the concerns of Jesus in a way that most missionaries had been unable to do.[32] Mao's lips have remained silent on naming the Name, but the Word is very much at work just the same. What we are confronting here is the distinction between a theoretical and a practical atheist. The former shows by his words that he does not believe in God, but his life bears eloquent witness to his harmony with God's purposes. The practical atheist, on the other hand, affirms by his words that he believes in God, but his life and priorities demonstrate what is the actual case.

This is to say, then, that the Judeo-Christian truths that are part of the mental lining of visitors are implicit in what is going on in China, setting up thereby a wavelength on which such meanings can be transmitted and received. When Senator Mansfield observed how people hang onto the words of Mao as if they were part of the gospel, he was uttering more truth than he may have realized. The verbal forms may differ, but the content is one of a kind in spirit and in thought. For example, Mao obtained the concept of a classless society from Marx, who in turn got it from Jesus. In the West it is known by the word "brotherhood," a teaching into which Jesus put teeth when he commanded his followers to call no man master, father, or rabbi, because in his way of thinking there was only one Master, one Father, and all others are brothers (and sisters) (Matt. 23:8–10). As most Protestants know, the Reformation doffed its Lutheran hat to this in the sixteenth century with its priesthood of believers doctrine, a concept that is still struggling to get off the drawing boards.[33]

Speaking in defense of both Marx and Jesus, it must be noted here that neither was unaware of innate differences among people.[34] The notion that we are all created equal is a myth unintentionally spawned by the Declaration of Independence.[35]

What both men, along with Mao, have sought to do is dispel the hostility and division that created differences foster if left unattended. We may not all be created equal, but we are all equally loved by the Creator. Consequently, the root cause of economic inequity is not the difference in ability, color, or sex, but the refusal of many human beings to take seriously the teachings of those who would have us work to eliminate the inequity the differences cause. Equity, domestic and worldwide, supersedes creation, or is the present phase of both creating and redeeming activity.

Another example of how the teachings of Jesus are implicit in those of Mao is in the directive concerning leadership. In a collection of his quotations he decries leaders who boss the masses around and emphasizes the need to be their friend—and indefatigable teacher, not a bureaucratic politician.[36] Jesus urges the same quality of leadership when he commends those who function as servants and laments gentiles who lord it over others (Matt. 20:25–26). In practical terms what this means is that the role of the servant in working for a classless society is to encourage the workers to become the managers. The separation between decision-maker and worker, which in ecclesiastical terms is clergy and laity, must be eradicated if creative power and initiative are to be set free.[37]

One other area is that concerning priorities. They are talked about in most Western pulpits but practiced in today's China. "Seek first God's kingdom and justice, and food, clothing, and shelter shall be yours as well," Jesus informed his disciples.[38] It's true that Mao has not revealed an awareness that it is God's kingdom he is seeking, but there can be no doubt that in making dignity for the oppressed and mutual regard for each other top priorities in Chinese society he is in effect placing God's kingdom first; in consequence, as God promised, food, clothing, and shelter have become available in ample proportion. Other by-products of the gospel emerge, such as a purpose for work and a community of which the majority feel a part. When cooperation is the national goal, the people live and work in an atmosphere that breathes goodwill into human relationships, instead of ill will.[39]

At this point a potential danger for China surfaces. Once the necessities of life are met, people can begin to hanker after other things, thereby losing sight of the initial priorities that made them strong. Rather than eat to live, they live to eat. Rather than work for a good reason, they work to be free from work. Luxuries become necessities, and these other priorities produce other results, less beneficial in the long run. Presumably in the ingenuity and effort expended to gain the necessities there is an "apple tree." Not to fall for it will take some sustained discipline on the part of the Chinese.

For now though, when one considers the kind of concerns that preoccupy the people and their leaders, one discovers that Another Gardener is at work. Although God's ordained means of identification were sent away, the kind of activity to which God has revealed a long-standing dedication suggests that he remained behind to work there, without a visa. We cannot nationalize God, for neither time nor space are barriers to him the way they are to us. It would appear axiomatic that wherever people share his priorities, there he too is involved.

Support for this assertion comes through Jesus and represents a major belief in the Western mind. God was in a position of lofty repute when B.C. became A.D. To change this image, Jesus, the Word, assumed human form. Although the "on high" deity persisted in the thinking of most and Jesus went about unrecognized, among those who did see there was awe and excitement. The thought of God with us inspired faith and service. Incarnational magnetism was at work.

Once again in China we see this kind of activity going on. In the first months of the Cultural Revolution professional and managerial persons did not take kindly to working alongside peasants and laborers. But the very act of doing so began to engender a spirit of enthusiastic cooperation among participants. What our understanding of Jesus tells us is that when persons of social, economic, political, or ecclesiastical prominence shed their aloofness and join the people in their struggle to live, they find a power within them that was not there before. This power is God's activity made apparent in Jesus Christ. However, with or without awareness of it, this activity contains a faith and a spirit that moves mountains.

The Bible even provides a mirror for reflecting on some of the more knotty images that no doubt lurk in the minds of visitors, such as that of thought control, otherwise known as brainwashing. The image that is conjured up is that of a person alone in a room bombarded hour after hour with propaganda from a loud speaker three feet away, as if by vocal power one could be given a new frame of mind.

In fact, visitors discovered that thought remolding goes on in two other manners. One is in discussion of Mao's teachings. Everyone has a copy of his book, and farmers meet two evenings a week to discuss it, while factory workers assemble in small groups three afternoons a week. Everyone cannot read, but all who can talk can think and do so aloud together. It puts meaning into the day. This is part of Mao's faith in the ability of the people to respond. Scheduled discussion is one secret of the Chinese experiment. The other means of thought remodeling is the "May 7th School." It takes place in the country amidst pig-raising, rice-planting, and KP. An American who visited one of these likened it to a summer camp in the U.S. and the cadres with whom he spoke sounded—and looked—as though they had lived through a soul-saving religious experience.[40]

Once again religious terminology is utilized to describe an atheistic activity. Once again the activity so described is not without biblical contact. We are referring to the exhortation of Paul that we be not conformed to this world but transformed by the renewal of our minds (Rom. 12:2). Thinking and rethinking, the dynamic in any and all genuine conversion, plays a large part in Paul's theological response to the gospel. It becomes the way to assimilate content, to digest it and make it one's own. This kind of activity is going on in any Christian church worthy of the name and the heritage. To visitors brought up on a diet of sermons in the U.S.A., this form of communication may have looked very good; to those who know, it was the Way of the Word in the first century.

ROBIN HOOD THEOLOGY

Having sounded this note, it would be erroneous for the reader to assume that everyone in China is in agreement with this biblical-socialist way of thinking. There are some, members of what was the Chinese aristocracy, who are now in labor camps. However, before one responds to this by thinking, "That's communism for you," it would be well to recall that it was Jesus who told the parable of Dives and Lazarus, the rich man and the beggar (Luke 16:19–31). His purpose evidently was to warn the rich of this world that the chasm between them and the poor is extended to the next life, but that tables are turned there. Actually, the former Chinese aristocrats and landlords are better off than the rich in Jesus' parable. The Diveses of China have the chance to improve their position. All they have to do is to accept the fact that the peasants are also human beings, and they can assume their place in society beside them. The rich in Jesus' story are in a fiery hell and the judgment is final; God is eternally on the side of the poor. The rich have no chance.

The note of futility in this story is perplexing. Jesus explicitly states that the words of warning have no effect in this life, no matter who brings them. What this suggests is that another approach is necessary, one that may include pressure or force. The story attributes to God a kind of Robin Hood image, especially wherein the positions after life are reversed. With this as the inevitable eventual outcome, the possibility that God might be doing some of this in this life already is a real possibility.

The only problem with the Robin Hood activity is whether robbery is an accurate word to describe it. From the point of view of the rich it would be, for they feel entitled to their wealth, often regardless of how they got it. From the point of view of the poor, however, robbery is not the right word. If a starving man watches another man eat his fill and then put the leftovers in a refrigerator, the starving man is entitled to that stored food. In fact, it belongs to him;[41] he is within his rights if he takes it. Thus, robbery is the correct term only if Dives is entitled to his affluence. If he is not, then taking it is not a crime. Keeping it is.

As to the use of pressure to bring about justice, if it is wrong in this life, then how can it be right in the next? On the other hand, if it is right in the next life, then how can it be wrong in this one, especially for God?

It has been my privilege to become acquainted with the farmworkers' cause in America. What has never ceased to amaze me is hearing the supermarket executives and the growers maintain that the laborers in the fields who work all day in the hot sun for poverty-level wages are exploiting the situation by the boycott of lettuce and grapes. That it does not occur to the grower or the grocer that he has been exploiting the farmworker for decades (as have we, the consumers) is astounding. That he has, however, and that the time has come to right this wrong, is inescapable.

When Patty Hearst renounced the life of luxury and her millionaire parents, in favor of the hard, desperate life of a rebel hunted by the police, two things stood out—one the change that took place in her thinking, the other the effect this had on certain people. "I have become conscious," she said in a taped message to her mother and father. "Love doesn't mean the same thing to me anymore." Her love was now filled with the knowledge that "no one is free until we are all free."[42] This amounted to the conversion of Dives' daughter. What is frightening in this case is the threat the powers-that-be felt from this one young lady. Millions were spent to capture her, so committed are the powerful to perpetuating the position of Dives in this world, and so oblivious are they to the implications in this story of Jesus.

When it comes to a fair, enduring, and equitable society, God and economics cannot be separated. Such was the conclusion to which the Roman Catholic Synod came in 1971. It observed that, in theory, Marxism "appears more attuned to God's plans than capitalist society." Although there are obvious distortions in the Marxist politico-economic system, the original model as conceived by Marx made "exploitation of man by man impossible or at least very difficult." On the other hand, the society that places capital at the center of everything and subjects man to the law of profit "commits a grave sin against the plan of God."[43]

In effect, the synod was saying that the economic system in which one is reared, or to which one is dedicated, can either help or hinder God's participatory activity—regardless of the faith of the citizen, one might add. An atheist in an ideal Marxist system would be in less danger of exploiting others than would a Christian in an ideal capitalist system. If an individual attempts to respond to the need to take others into account at the economic level, the Marxist will find it easier to do so through his society than will the Christian capitalist through his. It is impossible to implement justice in a system that depends on greed, but it is possible in a society structured for mutual concern.

ISSUES FOR DISCUSSION

1. Conditions at home make visitors to China receptive to what they see there.

2. Should China get tired of just meeting necessities and want luxuries, it will be a sign of progress.

3. We are all created equal.

4. In capitalism, as in sports, for every winner there are others who lose.

5. In a society dedicated to the survival of the fittest, the most God can do is comfort the afflicted and afflict the comfortable.

6. To extol free enterprise and then work to get a corner on the market is self-defeating.

7. Scheduled discussion is the secret of Chinese success.

8. God may end the prosperity of the rich at death, but he would not do such a thing before then.

9. The change in Patty Hearst may be called a conversion.

10. People who are materially poor are lazy.

NOTES

1. E.H. Johnson, "Challenge of the New China," *Church and Society*, January-February 1975, p. 5.

2. Ishwer Ojha, of Boston University, admitted that "China may be a poor country," but he reported one dominant impression. "It is a country that has abolished poverty" (See "31 Days in China," *Bostonia*, April 1972, p. 15).

3. Neville Maxwell, "The China Nixon Didn't See," *The American Scholar*, Autumn 1972, p. 547.

4. *Ibid.*, p. 556.

5. Robert P. Martin, "Life Is Earnest, and Rather Grim," *U.S. News and World Report*, March 13, 1972, p. 22.

6. "Inside Red China Today," *U.S. News and World Report*, May 29, 1972, p. 47.

7. "Peeking at Peking," *Boston Globe*, November 30, 1972.

8. Jonathan Mirsky, "A Sinologist in China," *Saturday Review,* July 1, 1972, p. 49.

9. *Ibid.*

10. Edward Klein, "China—Symbol and Substance,"*Newsweek,* March 26, 1973, p. 34.

11. Seth Kupferberg, "U.S. Students Get a Look at China,"*Parade,* October 6, 1974, p. 18.

12. Johnson, "Challenge," p. 7; Martin, "Life is Earnest," p. 22.

13. Scott, "Inside Red China," p. 49.

14. Mike Mansfield, "Inside Red China Today," *U.S. News and World Report,* May 29, 1972, p. 46.

15. Johnson, "Challenge," p. 8.

16. James Wallace Hamilton, *The Thunder of Bare Feet* (Westwood, N.J.: Revell, 1964).

17. Mirsky, "Sinologist," p. 47.

18. Otile McManus, "The Feverish Life in Chicago Trade Pits," *Boston Globe,* October 24, 1973.

19. "Can Capitalism Survive?" *Time,* July 14, 1975, p. 61.

20. Klaus Mehnert, *China Returns* (New York: Dutton, 1972), p. 81.

21. Mirsky, "Sinologist," p. 49.

22. Mehnert writes that the one criterion by which one can tell if a youth is a revolutionary is if he is willing to integrate himself with the broad masses of workers and peasants and does so in practice. If he is willing to do so and does so, he is a revolutionary; otherwise he is a non-revolutionary, or a counter-revolutionary. See *China Returns,* p. 291.

23. Mirsky, "Sinologist," p. 49.

24. Scott, "Inside Red China," p. 48.

25. Minority groups (see Johnson, "Challenge," p. 11) are from Tibet, Chuang, Hui, Lolo, Korea, and others.

26. Klein, "China," p. 34.

27. A significant historical parallel is the culture that flourished in India around 250 B.C., under the leadership of Asoka. Along with planting shade trees, digging wells, and building hospitals, he had simple reminders of the need for mercy, purity, and gentleness carved on pillars of stone and located where they could be easily read.

28. Mansfield, "Inside Red China," p. 46.

29. Scott, "Inside Red China," p. 49.

30. Johnson, "Challenge," p. 6.

31. Luke 3:4–6 sets Isaiah 40:4 in a context of social justice.

32. Johnson writes how helpless he felt as a missionary from 1935 to 1941 in the face of massive illiteracy, malnutrition, and corruption ("Challenge," p. 7).

33. John W. Dixon, Jr., notes that the doctrine of the priesthood of believers made scarcely any change in the clerical domination of church affairs. Today, despite greater participation by laymen, effective control is at every point still exercised by the clergy. See "Hierarchy and Laity," *The Christian Century,* October 25, 1967, p. 1353.

34. Both used the expression "each according to his ability," Jesus in a parable (Matt. 25:15) and Marx in a statement.

35. Ayn Rand bases her defense of capitalism on the idea that all people are "independent equals" (see *The Virtue of Selfishness* [New York: Signet, 1964], p. 31). She is correct in seeing this as the keystone of capitalism, but quite wrong in

accepting it as true. The founding fathers had equal rights in mind, not equal capacity.

36. *Quotations from Chairman Mao Tse-tung* (Peking: Foreign Language Press, 1972), p. 272.

37. "China and the History of Salvation," *Church and Society* (Report of Workshop 4 prepared for the LWF-PMV Colloquium on "Christian Faith and the Chinese Experience," Louvain, Belgium, September 9-14, 1974), p. 31.

38. Author's paraphrasing of Matt. 6:33.

39. The reporter who toured shops and sidestreets on his own wrote how people were "far more courteous than prior to 1949," when he had been there before. There was no pushing or shoving. See Martin, "Life Is Earnest," p. 49.

40. Klein, "China," p. 35.

41. Fr. James O'Donohoe, professor of Social Ethics of St. John's Seminary in Brighton, Mass., startled his audience in a local parish when he said this in 1973.

42. *New York Times,* April 4, 1974, p. 21.

43. Paul Hoffman, "Marxism Backed by Synod in Italy," *New York Times,* March 9, 1971.

CHAPTER 7

Light From Fort Jesus

In Kurt Vonnegut's novel *Cat's Cradle,* as darkness closes in on Bolivar, four of the characters are seated on a terrace overlooking a city. Light rises from several areas, and a visitor asks a resident what their points of origin are. There is the following exchange of words:

"House of Hope and Mercy in the Jungle, Papa's palace, and Fort Jesus."

"Fort Jesus?"

"The training camp for our soldiers."

"It's named after Jesus Christ?"

"Sure. Why not?"[1]

Vonnegut's satirical purposes demand that the question raised by the reference to "Fort Jesus" be left unanswered in the novel. But such a question is an open invitation to thought, for the words not only relate to the author's Bolivar, but also to modern America, where the image of a largely Christian nation and the policy of the Pentagon are not only incompatible, but diametrically opposed.

The satire is based on the presence of steeples and crosses pointing to heaven, on the one hand, and the interdependence between the economy and the military on the other. Each year the military side of this relationship surfaces when it comes time to justify the enormous amount of money allocated for defense. The Pentagon trots out charts to show how far ahead of us the U.S.S.R. is or how close behind us they are, thereby revealing its underlying weapon (or problem): fear. The military side also emerges with the announcements of multi-million-dollar spy planes, and electronic battlefields. Since no one expects that these are to be used here at home, they must, therefore, be intended for military purposes in other places. At least they are sold under that guise.

The economic side also comes through, as when it was disclosed some years ago that the United States and the Soviet Union had enough missiles stockpiled between them to kill every person on earth five times. Since a person can only die once, it is obvious that the continued missile build-up had—and still has—ceased performing a military function and become a means of promoting the economy. Recently, when reason and public pressure forced both nations' leaders to place a limit on the number of missiles, the U.S. economy was presumably threatened. At least the solution proposed by the government was to stabilize the quantity of missiles produced, but encourage the improvement of quality. The result was that rather than saving money, more money for defense could be poured into the economy, for research and for new manufacturing equipment. If one could take this seriously, one would have to perceive the way to peace not as converting swords into plowshares, but as building bigger and better swords. The real issue, of course, was not peace but prosperity.

The implication in this union of the military and industry is that peace would be a threat to national security. Some years ago, official Washington was embarrassed to have this thought published in "Report from Iron Mountain." The report concluded that we must have war because we could not economically afford peace.[2] Washington's response was to "play down" discussion of the report. It would seem, however, that whether this report was hoax or horror, the Pentagon does depend on war or the threat of war to stay in business, to justify its yearly allotment, to keep the military preoccupied and the manufacturers happy.

Perhaps one reason the Department of Defense is able to get away with the budgetary figure it submits to Congress and reports in the press each year is that the figure is so astronomical it almost defies comprehension, though not quite. Upon breaking the ninety billion down into one million dollar allotment checks, it assumes meaning and is sobering indeed. If one person were to receive such checks until the amount was entirely transferred to his account, he would have to live 246 years and receive it on the basis of one million dollars *a day* for that length of time.

If it were just a matter of providing jobs and income for people here at home the situation might be tolerable. However, because the products are military, and the expenditure enormous, the effect on the world at large and on our national psyche is devastating. Again, priorities produce results. Because the expenditure is thirty times what we spend to fight hunger, disease, and ignorance, the net result is not security, but insecurity, crime, and skepticism.

COUNTERPRODUCTIVITY

Fear is contagious. In some people it arouses the very reaction it is designed to offset. In the Soviet Union, for example, the fear of nuclear war led not to containment, but to incentive, and the missile race was on. In China, the effect was different. Nowhere is the care-for-people that nourishes its present policies more clear than in its response to the U.S.-U.S.S.R. missile race. Watching the build-up in America and in its own backyard, China took steps to assure the safety of its own people, something neither the U.S. nor the Soviet leadership undertook. Evidence to this effect was shown to Dr. Ojha during his visit to China, and he reacted with a mixture of surprise, awe, and depression. In the middle of a large department store in Peking, he was shown a button on a counter. When the button was pushed, the counter rolled away, revealing steps leading down, twenty-eight feet below, to miles and miles of concrete-brick tunnels. They support the entire city and can be entered from every department store, apartment building, and residence. In the event of a nuclear attack, Peking's seven million people could be safely in the tunnels in seven minutes and could walk through them to twenty miles outside the city. In every major city Dr. Ojha visited, he was shown these tunnels.[3] That the Chinese reaction to others' missile-building activity should simultaneously show the United States' lack of concern for its own people in heavily populated areas and China's abundance of concern, is the height of irony.

In America the results of our policy have been no less disconcerting than Ojha's discovery. Although the bill for military security is higher than the net income of all U.S. corporations, what we have gotten for our labor is economic disaster. Nothing is more inflationary than military expenditures. The military dollar may line even blue-collar wallets, but this money cannot be used by the worker to purchase his product. There is no market among civilians for tanks, missiles, and B-52s. Consequently, the military worker is alienated from his product, and his take-home dollars must be used for what can be purchased—housing, clothing, food, cars, luxuries. When there is more money chasing the same amount of goods, prices go up, and wages must do so also. Some get rich, but for the majority affluence is an illusion bought with the blood of their own sons. Granted the defense budget puts bread on many tables (and in many pockets), but it also removes a lot of plates.

As with any expenditure, somebody has to pay for it; in America it is the people who do so—in more ways than one. If our tax money were spent on constructive ventures it could add a purposeful dimension to our lives. But when the government takes an average of three months' pay from each worker's income and then uses 60 percent of that tax to destroy the lives and property of others, or to prepare for such activity, it harms the public conscience. It makes each taxpayer an accessory after the fact to homicide, and that does not cultivate a good feeling, even if the individual succeeds in suppressing the facts. Morale and morality suffer. Dishonesty becomes a sport, justified on the basis that "everyone's doing it" (even the president). Part of the tragedy is that the quiet, legal crimes of the rich lead to the overt, violent crimes of the poor.

From the biblical perspective, the most serious by-product of military-industrial security is what it has done to undermine belief in the teachings of God and Jesus. The thoughts that the teachings of Jesus arouse in relation to the use of military force have become locked in the subterranean recesses of the mind and access to them is guarded by the flag.

However, on two occasions that have come to my attention, the guard was momentarily lifted, and the truth emerged in analyzable form. One was when Tom Rodd was told that he was being sentenced to prison for the "preservation of society."[4] The other was when the candidate opposing Robert Drinan, a priest-dove running for Congress from Massachusetts, tried to discredit him by saying, "My heavens, this guy is a serious threat to the United States."[5]

Tom Rodd, it will be remembered, believed that love was the strongest force in the world; to have imprisoned him for relating this to the draft, the judge must have believed that love was weak and unsafe as a way of life. Similarly, if anyone thinks that a person who takes Jesus' teaching on peace seriously is a threat to the United States, he must believe that these teachings are either dangerous or naive.

Of course, neither the judge nor the politician explicitly referred to Jesus as a threat or as naive, but these assumptions are implicit in their statements. If one believes that force is the answer, one must have decided, consciously or unconsciously, that other answers are wrong and that those who espouse them, including Jesus Christ, are wrong too.

If a Christian American removes the flag and lets the light of consciousness delineate some of these underlying assumptions, he will find thoughts like the following taking shape. The image of Jesus is that of a eunuch whose chamber is the church. Alongside the military brass he looks weak and otherworldly; the only service he can perform for the Pentagon is to apply tourniquets and pronounce last rites. On the battlefield, he would surrender rather than resist the enemy. When men's backs are against the wall, he is a bleeding heart who is content to hang on a cross. Buried in the subconscious of the Joint Chiefs of Staff is the feeling that Jesus is neither believable nor realistic, that he is, at heart, naive. He has his ideas about peace on earth and goodwill to men proclaimed in church, but in the chilly world they don't cut the ice.

The next assumption is, of course, that it is the task of the exponents of military persuasion to provide the would-be followers of Jesus with protection. In order to let them bask in his love and preach about heaven, the Pentagon must maintain superior power on the land, in the air, and on the sea. Jesus and what he stands for have become the sublime excuse for pursuing a policy that prepares for war. The unarticulated gospel of the Pentagon is that love is an error, force a necessary evil, and Jesus a detriment to national security.

THE GODFATHER IMAGE

Not only are the teachings of Jesus contrary to those of the Pentagon, they also seem contrary to one of the Old Testament images of God: the one governing the conquest of Canaan and many other events. That image was of a Godfather who made offers most of his people dared not refuse. Those that did suffered the consequences: 14,000 died from a plague on one occasion, and 24,000 on another.[6] God was reputed to be merciful, but he had a strange way of showing it. If you did not respond to the right hand of blessing, the left hand of anger came around and whipped the sheep into line, that is, those who were still standing. Among the Jews, surrounded by ever-threatening natural dangers and influenced by this image of their God, the threat and use of capital punishment became the standard penalty for violations of all sorts.[7]

Remnants of this kind of thinking persist to the present day. Notice that insurance companies label wind, rain, and snow "acts of God." And, indeed, more people are killed by natural disasters each year than by all the automobile accidents and acts of war put together. What we spent years doing in Indochina, it took but minutes for God—or Mother Nature—to perpetrate at the Bangladesh end of the Bay of Bengal.

Thus this Old Testament image suggests to some that God had indeed empirical footprints in the world. But I believe that reverence for life suffers a severe setback if the Life Giver is held responsible for natural disasters, especially if they are accepted as punitively designed. How can man be expected to take the Fifth Commandment seriously if the Law Giver is the prime offender, or free from its demands on the grounds of executive privilege.

As for the conquest of Canaan, the picture of a warlord is no easier to accept than that of a Godfather. Moreover, if military force is God's will now, then Henry Kissinger is in direct violation of it as he works to bring about détente between Israel and the modern Canaan—the Arab nations. (On the other hand, if reason and goodwill are God's ways, then Mr. Kissinger is in harmony with him, a partner in the pursuit of peace when he works for a peaceful settlement in the Middle East.)

If God is not a warlord, how then can we understand his support of the original conquest of Canaan, the conquest that has kept the Middle East in turmoil for so many centuries? It began with the Exodus and God's promise of a home to Israel. It became imperative to find a permanent location for this nation of vagabonds, and, unfortunately, the Canaanites were not willing to make room. (Whether it be in Palestine, China, Russia, or the United States, landholders are seldom willing to voluntarily share what they think is theirs.) One could say, therefore, that in order for God to fulfill his longstanding promise, he had to force the Canaanites to move over. In doing this he maintained a semblance of rapport with the people of Israel; however, he also went against his primary will.

My acceptance of God's use of force in this case is predicated on the assumption that neither Israel nor the people of Canaan would have understood a nonviolent approach to the problem. Even God must have at least some human support through which to work in order to effect his primary will. The validity of this assertion is historically confirmed by the fact that when Jesus approached Jerusalem in triumph, he paused outside the gates and, with tears in his eyes, lamented that the people inside did not know the things that make for peace (Luke 19:41–42). Sure enough, when they discovered that he was not a King Saul or a David, that he had no heart for military conquest, their support quickly faded.

The point is well made in the rock opera, *Jesus Christ Superstar*. Simon the Zealot suggests that Jesus lead a revolt against Rome. In lyricist Tim Rice's song, Jesus responds that neither Simon, nor the people, nor the Romans, nor the Jews, nor Judas, nor the twelve, nor the priests, nor the scribes, nor doomed Jerusalem itself, understand at all what power is. To this list one could add Russia and the United States.

For many people, the most disturbing element in communism has been its use of military force to achieve its purposes. "Wars of liberation" seem to bring freedom to some individuals only through death. This has been especially true of Russian communism. But it must be remembered that it was on this point that the comrades of Marx left his instructions behind and made those of Lenin the model for the movement.[8]

To "Christian" nations in the West, especially the United States, communism has been, therefore, a curse to crusade against. And as Christians have done on previous occasions, the methods they adopted to exterminate the foe were the same as those that made the foe so reprehensible.

Many of these actions have been undertaken in the name of God. And the image of the Old Testament God considered in this section is indeed of a God who liquidated his enemies. But, although the Bible does not satisfy all our questions about the Creator's link with natural disaster, what it does do is to convey, by way of Jesus, an image that makes it difficult to reconcile the two. The film *The Godfather* made this point graphically. Near the end, the son, who is taking over his father's role, has his own son baptized. As the water is being poured on the child's head, there are fast flashes showing the new godfather's henchmen carrying out "contracts." Thus: "In the name of the Father," and an opponent is killed by a machine gun; "of the Son," and another is blown up with dynamite; and "of the Holy Spirit," and a third who might have gotten in the way is disposed of. In this manner, the viewer sees the policies of the godfather and those of Christianity placed in dramatic contrast.

THE PRINCE OF PEACE

It is perhaps significant that the one writer in the Old Testament who saw God as a Prince of Peace was not certain that God was the one who ordered the executions after all. Isaiah's awareness, however, was rather vague. He reflected the beliefs of his time, noting that God strikes, smites, and afflicts, but he seemed momentarily puzzled that God would do this to one who "has borne our griefs and carried our sorrows" (Isa. 53:4). He was not sure God should be seen in this light, but he had no other light by which to see. Thus, his insight had no more force than that of a passing thought.

In the New Testament this uncertainty was removed. God was seen in a new light: in the light of Christ. Famine, calamity, and war may slaughter us like sheep, but nothing can separate us from the love God demonstrated when Jesus died for us (Rom. 8:35–39). Some theologians would have us believe that Jesus somehow changed God's mind, that Jesus' atonement satisfied God's wrath, but according to the thought of John and Paul, God was in Jesus from the beginning (John 1:1–3; 2 Cor. 5:19). He was with him all the way. What Jesus suffered, God too bore. Moreover, when God demonstrated his approval of what Jesus taught and did by raising him from the dead, he was not just exercising a creator's prerogative. He was also making it impossible for us to conceive of the deity as holding a cross in one hand and a bayonet or switchblade in the other. The issue comes down to whether there is a split between the will of God and the will of Jesus, or whether they are one. Since the latter is the New Testament witness, the split then is between the will of God and the will of man, not between God and Christ.

In the light of the New Testament, we can no longer see God as a warlord, vindicating honor by defeating opponents militarily, for rather than inflict suffering upon others, he took our suffering upon himself. He does not delight in an eye for an eye but instead loves his enemies (Matt. 5:38–48). Paul translates this insight into what amounts to a foreign policy or a way of heading off international conflict. "If your enemy is hungry, feed him; if he is thirsty, give him drink; for by so doing you will heap burning coals upon his head."[9] By helping to meet a person's need for life's necessities, the envy and anger that makes him bellicose is consumed. Thus, the most effective preventive, the strongest deterrent to war is to undermine or to eliminate the cause for it. The Pentagon is doomed to failure because it seeks to put out fire with fire. Jesus would have us put it out with water—the most obvious, practical, and commonsense approach possible. Thus, Christianity is not a religion to be protected by military might. It is not a religion at all. It is God's revelation of how to cope with reality. It is the Way to relate to other people. It treats causes, not symptoms, and there is really no alternative that can succeed or that has succeeded.

This is the policy to which God is dedicated and is able to give full support. It is one to which Isaiah referred explicitly when he observed that when God had achieved justice in the land there would be peace. Isaiah's reference to the conversion of swords into plows indicated a connection between justice and peace; stated in plain terms, the connection is peace *through* justice.

A modern witness to the validity of this policy came from the lips of President Dwight David Eisenhower. After years in the military and eight more in the White House, he said:

Every gun that is made, every warship that is launched, every rocket that is fired signifies, in the final sense, a theft from those who hunger and are not fed, those who are cold and are not clothed. This world in arms is not spending money alone. It is spending the sweat of its laborers, the genius of its scientists, the hope of its children.[10]

THE ONE TRUE SAFEGUARD

Disarming Fort Jesus is the one true safeguard and it begins when, convinced that the Almighty is speaking through Jesus and other voices, we rely on their witness. We read in Solomon that as our ways please the Lord, the Lord will make even our enemies to be at peace with us (Prov. 16:7). Here is both the reason and the incentive to make certain that our priorities and our policies are in agreement with those that God has set forth. We put our faith in his promise to us, rather than in our nose-coned hardware, for the latter is a symbol of disbelief. We opt for giving plates of rice, not a menu of missiles. In other words, we do what we stamp on our coins, what we profess on Sunday: We trust in God and take Jesus seriously.

Trusting God does not, however, mean sitting back and waiting for him to act. God has already acted in Christ and the prophets; trust sees what he has said and done through them as worth continuing. Hence the next move in this reciprocating relationship is ours. That move must be to dismantle our missiles, to eliminate our warheads—both metallic and human—and to announce to the world that we are embarking on a new course, one that no nation has tried before, but one that has long been recommended by the Creator himself, one that he has promised to support. Trust in God means more than just a ten-billion-dollar cut in the annual defense budget. That is nothing really radical. Trust in God means to follow through with the antiwar thinking that emerged during the war in Vietnam, to transfer our funds from war purposes to peace purposes, from swords to plows. It means no less than the disarmament of Fort Jesus—or rather changing it to the "whole armor of God" which the gospel of peace uses as equipment (Eph. 6:10–17). It would be the first real "leap of faith" that any nation ever really took.

In the room in which this book was written hangs a cartoon clipped from a newspaper, the name of which is unfortunately missing. Jesus and Richard Nixon are standing in front of the Capitol, and, with his arm around Jesus, Mr. Nixon is saying: "It's a great plan, Jesus. I really mean that, only you must understand my position. Why, if I tried to tell that to the public, they'd probably crucify me."

Implementing this policy, this plan, would mean sending seeds to a potential enemy. It would mean parachuting food to an actual enemy, one with whom we are already at war, rather than dropping bombs filled with nails and napalm. Jesus is well aware of enemies. What engages his mind, and what would engage ours if we took him seriously, is how to make them into friends. In so doing we would discover the things that make for peace. It is not a matter of disarming and then trusting atheists not to take advantage of us. It is a matter of substituting food for guns and thereby letting the Lord God go to work on behalf of all concerned. This would be not the end but the beginning.

Trusting in God means walking in the "Shoes of the Fisherman." Remember how in the novel of this name a new pope mortgaged the property of the Vatican and sold most of its treasures in order to send grain to a country suffering from famine.[11] That country in the story was China. Now I am very aware that the United States has provided economic assistance to people in need—more than has any other country—and it does have a Peace Corps and an Agency for International Development. Noble as such efforts may be, however, they are severely handicapped by the weight of our military machinery. Currently, less than one percent of our GNP goes to countries in need, and too often aid is given with political strings attached and/or in emergency situations. Military expenditures, on the other hand, represent twenty percent of the GNP.

To be sure, there are times when emergencies arise and handouts are necessary. What is unfortunate, however, is that need has to reach a crisis point, as in the case of the East Pakistan disaster, and threaten the stability of the world before our humanitarianism is aroused. But if financial and technological aid were our basic policy, such emergencies would be few and far between. As an ancient Chinese proverb puts it, if you give a man a fish, he'll eat for a day, but if you teach him how to fish, he'll eat for a lifetime.

As long as we fill the sky with warplanes, the seas with warships, and the fields with cannon, and give God loaves and fishes, goodwill toward men will be little more than a Christmas card greeting. He still does wonders, but not even the Almighty can make a bomb taste good. We lament that God doesn't do more to end war. We think that if he were truly good he would. Yet, what we are expecting is that he who is the Prince of Peace will make friends out of enemies through materials designed to destroy them.

The only foreign or domestic policy that God can participate in redemptively, the only one that can join justice and peace, abroad and at home, is one that builds bridges over which people can walk together. Meeting life's necessities for food, clothing, and shelter does this because all human beings can become hungry and cold. When we make these our priorities, we will cultivate trust, not fear, and we will spread a cure, not a disease. True power is not what produces fear. It is what produces trust. It is what takes the fear away.

ISSUES FOR DISCUSSION

1. "Fort Jesus" is an apt description of the United States.

2. Fear and trust produce the same results.

3. The Pentagon depends on war or the threat of war for its purposes.

4. Having money from income tax payments used for war or preparation for war harms the consciences of the taxpayers, or should.

5. The military policy of the United States is based on the assumption that the teachings of Jesus about love and peace are a threat to national security.

6. God is free from the demands of his own law on the grounds of executive privilege.

7. Christianity is not a religion but God's revelation on how to cope with reality.

8. Doing what we have stamped on our coins does not mean disarming Fort Jesus.

9. Not even God can make a bomb do what food can do in meeting the needs of an enemy.

10. True power is what takes fear away.

NOTES

1. Kurt Vonnegut, Jr., *Cat's Cradle* (New York: Dell, 1971), p. 127.

2. *Report from Iron Mountain* (New York: Dial Press, 1967). The author, one of a reputed fifteen-man study group that may have produced the work, was unidentified (see *U.S. News and World Report,* November 20, 1967, p. 48).

3. Ishwer Ojha, "31 Days in China," *Bostonia,* April 1972, p. 15. Dr. Ojha's discovery of these safeguards rather decidedly alters the popular Western image of the Oriental attitude toward expendability. The image of hordes of Chinese charging an enemy stronghold without regard for loss of life is a product of the precommunist period when the ruling aristocracy saw war as a way of reducing the surplus population.

4. See Chapter 5 above.

5. *Boston Globe,* October 21, 1970, p. 3.

6. The first punishment (Numbers 16) was because some protested living out of a suitcase for decades in the wilderness; the second (Numbers 25:1–9) was for unauthorized "ecumenical activity" of the men of Israel with the daughters of Moab.

7. For example, see Lev. 20:9, 10; 24:16–17. Death was the penalty for hitting or cursing one's parents, committing adultery, or taking God's name in vain.

8. We tend to associate Marx with Russia and the parade of missiles through Red Square, designed to bury us. Marx, in fact, never saw Russia, despised soldiers, and "hated all despotic states" (see Randall, *Communist Manifesto* [New York, Washington Square Press, 1971], p. 8).

9. Paul wrote this in Romans 12:20, but he quoted it from Solomon, Proverbs 25:21–22.

10. "Cross of Iron" speech, April 1953.

11. Morris L. West, *The Shoes of the Fisherman* (New York: William Morrow and Co., 1963).

CHAPTER 8

God's Global Village

I have forgotten who it was who calculated, some years ago, that if the world were a global village of one hundred people

seventy would be unable to read;
one would have a college education;
fifty would suffer from malnutrition;
eighty would live in substandard housing by U.S. standards;
six would be Americans and they would have over half the town's
    entire income.

Today we should no longer need such a scaled down view to know of our relation to other people on earth. We may live on continents separated by water, but no longer and never more will we be separated from what happens on them. The eyes and ears of the world see and hear everything from hunger cries in Biafra to the bounce of a ping-pong ball in Peking. It's a small world after all, thanks to a network of international communications and the growing number of modest people, technicians, whose work and sense of urgency cross national and continental boundaries. Alberto Lleras Camargo, former president of Colombia, has observed that they are doing more to create a world suited to the needs of humankind than all the treaties ever signed by people in diplomatic attire.[1]

That this network of humanity should be operational in the sixties was certainly appropriate, for the decade ended with the sight of two earthlings walking on the moon with the nonchalance of masqueraders at a lawn party. It was a great leap for humanity partly because an estimated five hundred million persons saw it on television. It was truly a world event, although the United States served as host. It prompted moon parties in Lisbon, deserted streets in Prague, prayers in Rome, and 50,000 radio listeners in Zambia (but silence in China).[2] The moon not only belongs to everyone, but reaching it made our differences seem minor by comparison, our stupidities all the more intolerable. It was a poetic moment which Archibald MacLeish expressed in words worth recalling. "To see the earth as it truly is, small and blue and beautiful in that eternal silence where it floats, is to see ourselves as riders on the earth together, . . . brothers who know now that they are truly brothers."[3]

The event was like a seed. The impact of the moment may have died, but not without having added new shoots to our global consciousness. More are contributed by the youth of the planet every four years. Olympic competition is intense, but neither it nor tragedy can smother the international feeling that permeates the news and the Olympic Village where the athletes eat and live together. In 1972 this spirit reached such proportions that even many American viewers were embarrassed during the opening parade when the United States flag was not lowered as a courtesy to the host country. For Olga Connolly, the one carrying our flag, it was painful. "Had we lowered it," she declared, "it would have said that we do not consider ourselves above any other country. It would have said we are of the same Olympic faith; . . . we are all made of the same dough."[4]

In response to the pressure she and others exerted, she was finally allowed to lower the flag during the giving of the Olympic oath. At that moment we acknowledged that we are but one set of residents on the planet earth. We do not own it or control it.

It would, however, be unfair to praise or to blame science and technology alone for this mind-expanding period in history. Technicians are the visible workers, but here, too, there is reason to call attention to the activity of the Creator. In the first century, Paul had no knowledge of transoceanic cables or interplanetary spacecraft, but he did bear witness to God in terms that speak to such achievements. In the midst of the hundreds of idols in Athens, he noticed an empty altar, with the inscription, "To an unknown God." Presumably the prevalence of so many man-made images came from an indigenous discontent with what they represented, a discontent that was quietly epitomized in the barren shrine. What they worshipped as unknown he proceeded to describe as the Unseen One in whom we live and move. Then he observed that this God had created every race from one stock, fixing the epochs of their history and the boundaries of their territory (Acts 17:22–26).

To adhere to Paul's sense, two things must be said in rapid sequence. One, God determines man's limits, and we are indeed bound by them. The other, if humanity seems to be entering new territory, it would follow that those limits are farther than we realized. It is also in order to say that the dawn of this global consciousness is, to borrow a phrase from Alexander Graham Bell, something "God has wrought," through the efforts of technicians and others. We are living in a fullness of time once again. The Almighty has known all along that twenty percent of the population possesses eighty percent of the wealth. Now, with radio, TV, and telephones, we know too. The knowledge that was God's alone is making us more than ever aware that we are members, not only one of another, but of a global village as well.

In this chapter I shall underscore the Gardener's international activity in that village. Isaiah said that the government rested on the shoulders of a Son, and that it would extend to all nations. Since this Son is also Mighty God, Everlasting Father, he has no office, no headquarters. The town hall may be located on Manhattan Island, but the Unseen Comptroller is not confined within its walls. In God's jurisdiction, presidents, premiers, and chairmen are but precinct captains, although they, too, participate in his activity.

HORIZONTAL RECONCILIATION

The kind of activity to which God is dedicated includes that which changes enemies into friends. Fifty some years ago Germany was defeated in war and the peace terms were without mercy for the vanquished. When Germany had to be subdued a second time, the victors demonstrated compassion. Each policy was one the "enemy" remembered, but where in the first case it resulted in the desire for revenge, in the second it made them our friends. The biblical term for it is reconciliation, and a similar dynamic won over Japan, following its defeat in World War II.

Cold wars present the need for reconciliation also. The word "détente" has room in it for this dynamic, and contemporary history shows signs of God at work, not just with regard to the superpowers, but with lesser powers as well. It might seem that between East and West Germany blood would run thicker than water. However, it has taken more than nationality to open up the Berlin wall. It has taken trust and friendship.

Though it always seems that fighting is going on somewhere, or the threat of it, most of the world is at peace, and this is not to be lightly regarded, even if it does not make the newspapers. The prayer of Jesus that his disciples might be one has international as well as ecclesiastical overtones. Then, too, the incarnation news that God has taken up residence in humanity keeps a Christian's thoughts about reconciliation in a horizontal dimension. Indeed, properly understood, the gospel message lays the vertical dimension to rest; what remains, as fruits of the Spirit, are such categories as personal and social, in contrast to up, down, or sideways. Christians are again beginning to understand that to speak of "God's relation to man" and "man's relation to man" as if they were unrelated is to convey the impression that God is part only of the first relationship. In reality, humans are related to God just as much through love for others as through faith in divine forgiveness. God is at work in all, through all, and for all, so in reconciling the world to himself, he also reconciles people to each other.

In those places on earth where hostility seems always to bubble beneath the surface, such as in Northern Ireland and the Middle East, there has been bad blood for a long, long time. Change there is slower. However, the pressure of world opinion can be seen as God's human nudge. Truth becomes an international force. What people do to people in Hungary, or Vietnam, or in South Africa becomes the concern of people in many other nations also.[5]

Moreover, when enemies begin to cooperate, one is encouraged to think of the Prince of Peace changing swords into plows, of people responding to his priorities. Indeed, social cooperation is the active consequence of efforts toward reconciliation. For example, in 1970 the president of the United States spoke to the United Nations concerning areas in which our country and the U.S.S.R could cooperate, areas such as "peace," "reduction of arms," "environmental control," "trade and commerce," and "relieving the needs of the world."[6] Since this address, plans for such cooperation have been implemented. These two superpowers have signed agreements for joint projects such as cancer and heart disease research. In late 1970 a space rescue pact was signed, under which either country is allowed to rescue the other's spacemen. To make this possible they agreed to standardize future spacecraft so that ships of both nations could dock in orbit; in July of 1975 this experiment was successfully carried out. Since every inhabitant of the global village is a citizen of the solar system, the next step will be to pursue such ventures through the 28-nation committee of the U.N. General Assembly, set up in 1959 to study peaceful exploration of outer space.

Cooperation is not to be disparaged wherever and whenever it takes place, for within it can be the dynamics of friendship. We have already seen the first overtones of this since President Nixon's visits to Peking and Moscow. In September 1973 the Soviet government ceased jamming the Voice of America, making it possible for tens of millions to tune in each night. When the table tennis team of the People's Republic of China played an exhibition match in Detroit, the American and Chinese flags were side by side on the wall. And the Michigan State band played "Hail to the Victor" when China won the match five to one. But the point at which viewers got goose bumps was when the players left the arena. In pairs, one American and one Chinese, they clasped hands and raised them high together before the camera. One announcer remarked, "Here's an incongruity." Actually, it was his comment that seemed out of place. The young people to whom he referred were a bit older than the ones Jesus said we should emulate in order to enter the kingdom, but they were demonstrating the openness, the eagerness to grow that such children have. They were "put in our midst" and they were "leading us," just as Jesus and Isaiah had said children would be and do.

Once this stage in a new relationship has been reached, it becomes difficult to revert to prior levels of animosity, or even to maintain profound and fundamental differences, for what people have in common takes on fresh importance. When the ecumenical movement led to conversation and cooperation, it created a climate in which motives for doctrinal differences came under serious scrutiny. Roman Catholics' deeply cherished belief that theirs is the "one true Church" could no longer be held over the heads of Protestants when the doorway to "getting to know you" had been thrown wide open. Even the phrase "separated brethren" began to seem out of place in light of the new rapport.

What God began in the Church in the sixties is being felt in the world in the seventies. The prophecy of an Egyptian professor of surgery appears to be sound. "I am ... convinced," said Mohammed Mamel Hussein, speaking at the U.N. in 1965, "that in a few years' time, there will no longer be any talk of thermonuclear war. People will wonder what the scare was all about. ... The degree of hatred ... between nations will have to reach red heat before such a war is waged, and this will never take place once people work together peacefully and usefully."[7]

GLOBAL INTERDEPENDENCE

Those whose faith is reinforced by a military ideology laugh at the suggestion that friendship has induced the Soviet regime to cooperate. They believe that the atheist lacks the inner capacity for genuine friendship; all his motives are suspect, and any action that appears to be friendly cannot be trusted. Washington hawks would like us all to believe that it is the billions we have spent in the arms race that have ushered in the détente and made cooperation or coexistence a necessity.

But while the Pentagon was counting its warheads, a growing number of alert human beings began to realize a number of nonmilitary factors that carry an urgency all their own. Awareness of the threat of national destruction came with awareness of the potential of the bomb, but awareness of the threat of human extinction came with awareness of polluted air, poisoned water, food shortages, and dwindling supplies of natural fuel. The missile race resulted in a standoff, but the threat our damaged ecology poses is drawing people together. It has made cooperation a necessity. (Ironically, the holocaust with which nature is threatening earth would have arrived with or without the billions spent on nose-coned hardware.)

In June 1972, the member-states of the U.N. gathered in Stockholm in search of a formula to protect and restore the environment. One blueprint for global cooperation urged setting up a network of stations to be called "earthwatch" to monitor air pollution around the planet. That all nations attending this Conference on Human Environment did not agree is secondary to the fact that so many were joined together to solve a mutual problem. There will be more meetings on this subject. This was but the first of its kind.

When the Arab oil embargo produced long lines at U.S. gas stations in the winter of '73–'74, it also produced in some the feeling that we might have to invade Arab territory and take over the pumps. This dissipated, however, with the realization that American refineries were using the embargo for their own purposes, and that in Europe the cost of fuel has long been sky high. Presumably, if there is to be a leveling of the affluent mountains, if the wealth of the world is to be more equitably distributed, economic pressure will play a part. Standards of living become set, and it requires shock therapy to lower them, or even to raise them in some cases. What we are really up against though, in the energy crisis, is the Creator's distribution of the resources. No man and no nation is an island, and this goes for the Arabs as well. The United States cannot now survive without their oil, but the Arabs cannot bring down the economy of the West without destroying their major source of income.[8]

As if to remind us that neither human nature nor technology is totally to blame for the world's ills, Mother Nature kicked up her heels during '73–'74. Farmers in India looked in vain for the monsoon rains, upon which they depend for good crops. In Africa, even ancient water holes dried up. Drought and death settled over much of the Third World. As so often happens during adversity, with news of the food shortage on the front page, nations gathered together—this time in Rome—to decide what to do about it. Two issues were raised and introduced into the general public's consciousness. One had to do with the ethics of food relief, the other with the ethics of abundance.

In a time when food is short and human population itself has become a problem, do you feed people who are unconcerned about controlling it as well as those who are doing something about it? In spite of government efforts to educate the masses in India, they have thus far rejected family planning. What do you do when people refuse to see the handwriting on the wall, when feeding them can actually make matters worse?

The year 1973–74 reminded people in the Third World of their need to control births; it also saw those of us in capitalist lands, such as the U.S., learning that we must control our appetites. Various kinds of communications told us that we were literally taking food out of the mouths of those who were starving.[9] They depend upon grain, we upon meat; much to our dismay, we learned that it takes five to eight pounds of grain to produce one pound of meat. Is it moral to use scarce food to fatten livestock if, when fed directly to humans, it would feed five to six times as many people? And, as if it was not embarrassing enough to learn that an American family of four eats five times what an Indian family of eleven eats, it was more disconcerting to hear that we do not need to eat that much—in fact, it may not be healthy for us to do so. We consume more meat than our bodies can use, thereby draining excess protein off into the septic tank or sewer, and we are no healthier than the British, the Swedes, or the Japanese, who consume much less meat. And now some experts are suggesting that the prevalence of cancer and heart disease in America is caused by excessive consumption of beef and pork.[10]

Economic necessity has reared its head here too. As I write it costs more to raise livestock than they are bringing at the market. The time has come, it would seem, to reduce the intake of animal products and to increase the production of agricultural products. But even increasing agricultural output also has economic overtones. Americans put more fertilizer on their lawns and golf courses than is used by all the farmers of Hindustan. And by depriving farmers in the Third World of their supply of fertilizer they have unwittingly raised their need to import grain, thereby inflating grain prices here at home.

The most recent in the series of international meetings was one held in New York City, in late November 1974: "The Energy Outlook and Global Interdependence." At this conference, Ambassador Eishara of Kuwait expressed an awareness that sums up the feelings of many: "We cannot enjoy prosperity in the midst of hunger," he said. "We cannot be opulent in the midst of poverty. If we do, international security will be beyond reach."[11]

Robert McNamara, president of the World Bank, recently concluded an article in the *Saturday Review* with the thought that 1974 will be remembered as the year when the word "interdependence" stopped being rhetoric and started being reality.[12] To the degree that rhetoric has to do with verbal communication, it is not all bad. Prior to the Rome Conference and the worldwide attention it received, the above facts were realized only by scholars and field workers. Now they have taken their disturbing place in our world view, and we can hardly be the same.

How does the overall theme of this book relate to humanity's new realization of its interdependence? That humanity should be drawn together in the face of threats does not come from the survival instinct alone. Had the possibility for cooperation not been present, had it not been built into the fabric of human relationships, there would have been no alternative to self-destruction. We are indebted to Jesus Christ that this possibility existed. Through him and for him, the New Testament says, the world was not only created, but holds together (Col. 1:15–20). The priority policy of bearing one another's burdens and mutual helpfulness, which he revealed through his teachings in the first century, is but a reflection of the only way the world can effectively proceed; in a world community, where the interests of others must be taken into account in order to preserve one's own, it is inevitable that we should be moving in that direction. There is no other alternative, no other way. Through him, whether or not we recognize it, human beings are able to rise above the catastrophies of nature and find a common bond in our lives together.

DIVINE RESTLESSNESS

One of the more certain empirical signs that a new world is waiting offstage is the unrest that is felt in many corners of the global community. Socio-economic eruptions are occurring, and, in some places, sweeping changes have been made.

No country is immune to this unrest. Workers in Sweden, for example, arrived at a point where they could no longer endure the mind-destroying work on the automobile assembly line; with labor turnover pushing 100 percent, Saab, for one, decided to do something about it. Four-man teams now assemble entire engines, rather than one man having to stand in one place all day and tighten bolts. The result has been the humanization of the production process.[13]

In France and Canada, the nineteenth-century concept of the employer being absolute master in his own house, accountable only to stockholders, is under extreme pressure. In France the second largest trade union federation has demanded worker self-management, and in Quebec the Confederation of National Trade Unions has called for the creation of an industrial system, controlled, managed, and even owned by workers.[14] It is not necessary for the profits to be absorbed by a few for the corporation to function. Everybody but the super rich would be ahead if gains were shared more equally. This would replace individual competitiveness with group incentive.

Chapter 5 described how the unrest students found in parents made the thoughts of Karl Marx more than academic. In recent years this unrest has lead to some minor changes here in the United States. In Topeka, Kansas, for example, efforts are being made to treat workers as mature, responsible adults. General Foods is trying to share status and responsibility by eliminating reserved parking space for executives, basing office area on need and not on rank, banishing time clocks, abandoning the posting of in-plant behavior rules, and putting the same carpeting in locker rooms as on rug row.[15]

Unfortunately, in America there is a hurdle in the course toward equalization that is not present in China. In China the disparity is—or was—between rich and poor Chinese; in America it is between classes plus between those of different skin color. The U.S. is a microcosm of the world community. It is one of the corners of the global village where races are not separated by natural boundaries, a land to which all continents have contributed representatives. At times this in fact has brought the melting pot to a boiling point, but in due time the brew will be a good one.

In America, capitalism (alias free enterprise) has been the hardest on blacks, reds, and uneducated whites, for it expects them to rise above limitations their affluent neighbors never confronted. Take away an adequate job, education, and decent housing, and you have three strikes before you even come up to bat.[16] Try to escape through television and you are reminded just how nice others have it, a reminder that can further sap incentive to try. Welfare can become a way of life, but it, too, destroys initiative and self-esteem. Opponents of the bussing programs say it is a very complicated issue, even though many students have been relying on public transportation for years. Proponents of bussing for racial equality see it simply as that, though they do not relish the thought of their children going to a hostile neighborhood either. Proponents can be white parents as well as black. What they have in common is the vision that integrated education is an opportunity; it allows for getting acquainted at an early age, something to which most urban parents were never exposed.

Fortunately, the yeast is on the rise. A growing number of Americans are learning what the whole world will eventually discover, that beneath the surface there is one race after all. On the outside the color may be dark or light, but inside the color is human. Moreover, there is an unease at work in this land of the free which may very well lead to a more equitable relationship between people. I mean the uncomfortable feeling one can get from seeing black persons so often in a servant position, in relation to the rest of society. One may read or hear about blacks serving as gardeners, cooks, chauffeurs, and maids for the wealthy, but most whites actually see them in this role serving as red caps, shoeshine boys, elevator operators, and cleaning ladies. This is disturbing because the one who washed the feet of the twelve is at work here. In Jesus there is neither slave nor free.[17] We will not feel right about our relationship to other human beings until this biblical truth becomes empirical reality.

When we consider the underlying reason for the unrest in the souls of rich and poor, black and white, socialist and capitalist, we encounter the divine restlessness. Material gain is not the only factor that is at work in the minds of the poor. There is also a desire for dignity, purpose in work, and a sense of belonging to the group, concerns to which God revealed a commitment in both Jesus and the prophets. These are the qualities the German peasants of Luther's day and the Jerusalem segment of the first-century church found in the gospel.

It does not take a seer to see that men and women are finding it difficult to live with inequity. Karl Barth wrote that no relegating of our hopes to a Beyond can give us rest, for it is the Beyond itself standing outside and knocking on the closed doors of the here-and-now that is the chief cause of our unrest. Something tells me that Karl Marx would have cheered this idea. However, for Barth the unease is theistic in origin. It is given and thereby sustained by God, and we cannot escape it. Without wishing to, we must take part in an attack which is directed against the deepest foundations of society. "The onward march of God in history necessitates our advancing from . . . a naive acceptance to a criticism" of all social relationships.[18] When we find ourselves giving expression to such impulses, it is not we alone who are speaking, but also the One in whom all things persist is giving expression to his creative-redemptive purpose.

There are still many places in the Global Village where the strong dominate the weak and the rich exploit the poor. The meek have by no means inherited the earth—yet. However, I have been talking about the glimmerings of a planetary community, a new world coming, not one that has already arrived. It is only in one part of town that daylight can be seen, and there it has but dawned. Nevertheless, it would seem fair to conclude that we are living in one of those times when the boundaries are being pushed back, when the end of one period is giving way to another. In our history books, individuals with prophetic vision stand out like peaks on the plains, but today we seem to have an entire generation of prophets. The youngest shoots of humanity's family tree not only see very well but are supported by a convergence of forces that are confirming the reliability of their vision and helping to set in motion a legacy to their own children. What one man is to a fountain, most of today's youth are to a tide, though, as always, there are exceptions. It is just a matter of time before they have the numerical strength to vote in or otherwise influence the priorities needed to change the world. Considering the part youth played in the rejuvenation of China and in the thinking of Jesus, we can understand how Mao says, "Young people are like the sun at seven or eight o'clock in the morning."

ISSUES FOR DISCUSSION

1. Since attention given to space trips soon gives way to bread and butter concerns, they could hardly serve a unifying purpose in the psyche of the earth's people.

2. Paul's thoughts about God and boundaries have nothing to say to us today.

3. In reconciling the world to himself, God reconciles people to each other, even though they may not realize he is doing so at the time.

4. The pressure of world opinion is just that—world opinion.

5. God may be effecting détente in the Church, but in the world, between nations and peoples, that's another thing.

6. Self-preservation is no match for self-destruction.

7. What we are facing in the energy crisis is the Creator's distribution of resources designed to bring us closer together.

8. It is Christ who makes us uneasy about certain people always being in the servant position in society.

9. Today's youth represent a great hope for the world.

NOTES

1. Alberto Lleras Camargo. in an address at the inauguration of "International Cooperation Year," United Nations, New York, 1965.

2. *New York Times,* July 21, 1969, p. 10.

3. Archibald MacLeish, "The Year of the Moon," *National Geographic,* May 1969, p. 614.

4. *Boston Globe,* August 27,1972. Special story.

5. During the invasion of Budapest, hundreds of civilians were killed in the streets by Russian tanks and guns. Twelve years later in Prague, not a shot was fired. Perhaps one reason was that the pressure of truth had reached the Kremlin.

6. See Richard Nixon, *U.S. Foreign Policy for the 1970's* (Washington: U. S. Government Printing Office, 1970).

7. Mohammed Mamel Hussein, in an address at the inauguration of "International Cooperation Year," United Nations, New York, 1965.

8. An Arab Ambassador from Kuwait, at a convocation in New York in November 1974, said that the Arab nations were considering recycling petroleum funds to help avoid a "collapse of the Western economic system because this could amount to a breakdown of the world economic system" (*Boston Globe,* November 21, 1974, p. 6).

9. See, for example, Orville Freeman, "I Have A Plan," *Saturday Review,* December 12, 1974.

10. *Ibid.,* p. 13.

11. Further evidence that Arab leaders are aware of the need to be good stewards of their newfound wealth came through Hisham Nazir, head of Saudi Arabia's Central Planning Committee, when, in reference to the Cadillac era of the 1950s, he acknowledged, "We have wasted so much money" (Roberta Horning, *Brockton Daily Enterprise,* September 27, 1974, p. 25).

12. "Greening the Landscape," *Saturday Review,* December 14, 1974.

13. Donald White, "Humanizing the Assembly Line," *Boston Globe,* June 7, 1972, p. 29.

14. David Deitch, "U.S. Lags in Workers' Control," *Boston Globe,* June 16, 1972, p. 43.

15. *Time,* October 30, 1972, p. 97.

16. Forty percent of black families in the U.S. may own their homes, and the total black income may equal the GNP of India (see Lewis Foy, "An Optimist's Checklist," *Saturday Review,* December 14, 1974, p. 85), but for the majority, both domestic and foreign, life still spells i-n-e-q-u-i-t-y.

17. Gal. 3:28; Col. 3:11. Both slave and free are subject to the will of higher authority.

18. Karl Barth, *The Word of God and the Word of Man* (Grand Rapids: Zondervan, 1935), pp. 310–19.

CHAPTER 9

Thy Kingdom Come—on Earth

The theme of this final chapter is chronologically appropriate because the movement of history is forward and so is the movement of this book; what comes at the end is the fulfillment of all that has gone on before.

There are those who would have us believe that human society is on a free fall into the future, that the destiny of humanity depends entirely on us. They may be trying to panic people into a sense of responsibility, but they forget one thing in the process. There is no such thing as a free fall. Man may glide, dip, and float, but invariably he comes down to earth, because of something built into creation which we call the force of gravity. By a similar token, history may present surprises, new starts, dead ends, tragedies, and glimmerings of fulfillment, but there is an ultimate direction in which civilization is moving. The Creator has not relinquished his intention in Christ to reconcile all things to himself. In, with, and under the will of man is the will of One who said, "Behold, I make all things new" (Rev. 21:5).

The New Testament, by its very existence, bears witness to this newness, but our awareness of it can be remote as was that of Karl Marx. Remember that he was sufficiently impressed with the thought of a realm where brotherhood reigned supreme to use it as his model for society here on earth. Marx thought the idea was his own, and many of us think the same idea is nice but fanciful. What neither he nor most of us have realized is that it has been a part of human language for over nineteen hundred years, thanks to the words Jesus shared with his first disciples in response to their request "teach us to pray" (Luke 11:1). That the priorities of justice and peace should be ridiculed by the world's Archie Bunkers or by persons in positions of power is ironic, for many of these people in the West have verbally given God a green light to bring it all about. Sunday after Sunday, and frequently in between, they have prayed "thy kingdom come, thy will be done on earth as it is in heaven." Most would agree with Luther that there are two kingdoms, but for nearly two thousand years they have prayed that the one in heaven would become an earthly experience.

There is something uniquely disturbing about the look of surprise you so often get when you bring out the words "on earth" in relation to "thy kingdom come." To be sure, the sheer frequency of repetition dulls the mind to the meaning of the words. And having to say the Our Father as a penance is not exactly an incentive to comprehending the text. However, it also seems that most people see the kingdom of God as a kind of heavenly arrangement designed to bypass earth. They have probably drawn this conclusion subconsciously from the prevalent image of Jesus, seated on a celestial throne next to God and from the faith preoccupation with the need to "get there." Other petitions Christ recommended—about forgiveness, or temptation, or daily bread—have found their way into Christian content and conversation, but the one about the kingdom coming on earth has seldom registered in human minds.

This deeply entrenched image of a heavenly kingdom has not only caused most Christians to pass over its earthly counterpart in the prayer of Jesus. It has also shaped their interpretation of references to the kingdom that Jesus made at various times during his visible ministry. For example, when Jesus told Pilate that his kingdom was not of this world, he was not suggesting that it was in some other place, but that its origin was of God, and its priorities were, therefore, different (John 18:36). And when Jesus said the "kingdom of God is in the midst of you," he was not consigning it to a permanent state of mental reflection; he was simply designating where it must take hold (Luke 17:21). God's own integrity demands that, having promised the kingdom, he must seek to fulfill it here and now, as well as hereafter. Intermittently it shows itself in the discontent people feel over the way things are, but it does not fade the moment they begin to do something about their restlessness. What humans do on earth, whether they realize it or not, is their response to the one who spans the generations and cannot settle for less on earth than he knows to be his eternal plan.

In the human response to God and to his priorities there is the possibility—perhaps the inevitability—of distortion, especially when the one responding feels God has no part in the process. This can happen even with people who do have a belief in God. Consequently, in the U.S.S.R. today there is distortion of the ideas of Karl Marx, just as in Christian countries there is a distortion of the teachings of Jesus. For this reason many theologians are cautious about identifying the kingdom with any one political system or ideology. Many theologians, however, have been too wary of admitting that a movement might reflect God's influence, so a chasm has opened up between "God's world" and "man's world." We are left with the question that Teilhard de Chardin shared with Maurice Blondel in 1917: whether the work accomplished by nine-tenths of humanity during nine-tenths of the time, namely the building of the earthly city, has any meaning in relation to the kingdom of God?[1]

It does, but only in the context of justice, peace, and faith. If our efforts to build the earthly city elevate some people at the expense of others, we are merely reciting the Lord's Prayer, we are not praying it. A thirty-hour work week, free-moving highway traffic, ample supplies of gas, reduced hospital costs, and cable television that allows for in-home shopping would all be nice, but if other people are left out in the process of getting them, we do not see what God or many of today's youth see.[2] Remember that no chain, not even a human one, is stronger than its weakest link. For example, an apartment overlooking Central Park or the Boston Commons may be as luxurious as it appears, but how free are the occupants if they do not dare walk across the street at night? A large home in the suburbs may spell financial success, but does it truly represent success if the owner has to switch on his home-security system before leaving it? It would seem axiomatic that in America there is neither liberty nor justice for anyone until there is liberty and justice for all. To pray for the coming of God's kingdom is to be cognizant of this fact and to work for its coming.

It is necessary to note here that the earthly phase of God's kingdom is not another name for utopia. The latter in the male public mind conjures up the image of a year-round vacation from work, resting beside a swimming pool with a cool drink in hand watching the girls go by. In the skeptical technical mind utopia is a dream state, a human plan that never gets off the drawing boards; it never arrives for the masses. The kingdom of God that is built on justice and peace differs from utopia in several respects. First, it involves all human life on this planet, not just the life of a small group as in Skinner's *Walden II*.[3] Second, it does not signal the cessation of human effort as in the popular image of utopia. As long as there are people on earth, they will need food, clothing, and shelter, and they will have to work to obtain them. This means sweat and effort. Moreover, as the yellow pages suggest, people will always have to work to maintain and repair what they make with their hands. There is an inevitable obsolescence as well as a planned obsolescence. Even in a society where the service motive replaces the profit motive, where each person realizes that he is dependent upon his neighbor, human effort will be required. "We are not praying," writes J. Robert Nelson of Boston University, "for a utopia on earth, nor for a miraculous cessation of all man's ills and agonies. But we pray for . . . the secret drawing of men and women everywhere by their free assent into the significant life for which they have been created."[4] That is a place and a time where the priorities of God are those of humanity, where mutual cooperation makes possible not just the physical necessities, but meaning and purpose as well. The kingdom of God is just that. Along with the human effort is the activity of God whose work and Word inspires it.

In passing, it should be noted that God's kingdom on earth is not a substitute for that eternal fellowship into which we enter one by one. No matter what life on earth becomes, we will still live on borrowed time here. The victory over death and the grave that we see in Jesus Christ teaches us that death is the beginning not the end (John 11:23–26). But we do not know anything about our mode of departure from this life into another. No Christian can lay claim to any inside information on where heaven is or what goes on there, but no one can thereby disavow the existence of such a dimension or the inherent relationship between God and man that it promises. As long as people inhabit this planet, death will be the way of exit from the earthly phase of God's kingdom to the eternal one. Men may find cures for many diseases but the cure for death is neither desirable nor practical. In fact, had it not been for death, procreation would have long ago made life on earth impossible. Human beings do not need new myths to live with the reality of two kingdoms. They just need the faith that comes through sensitivity to the plain sense of Scripture and willingness to interpret pertinent passages in terms of the time when they were written and in terms of meaning for today.

What I am affirming in this book is that historical forces have helped change the theological issue from heaven and how to get there, to earth and how to live here, together. The kingdom for which we work and pray is simply a world where people care for each other, as well as for themselves, and where they acknowledge God.

THE ARRIVING KINGDOM
AND THE RETURNING CHRIST

It is crucial to my thesis to clarify what the above subheading signifies to me and how the thought of fulfillment relates to it. I am indebted to Carl Braaten and Peter Hodgson for making it possible for me to join together the kingdom of God and the return of Christ (the Second Coming), but I reserve the right to provide my own interpretation. Braaten refers to the "arriving kingdom," and Hodgson affirms that history is being pulled forward by the power of an arriving presence.[5] The issue here is one of direction, as stated in the chapter's opening paragraph. The thoughts of an arriving kingdom and a returning Christ convey the image of both being out there ahead of us, in space or in time, moving in our direction, and we in theirs, so that eventually there will be a kind of meeting or collision.

I find the terms arriving and returning meaningful, but only in the sense that God is with us now through Christ, though unrecognized, and that we are, together with him and because of him, moving forward to a time when he will be recognized for what he is and for what he has been doing. By way of analogy, picture a subway train running parallel to, but below, a freeway through a city. The train proceeds unknown to the passengers in the automobiles above, until at a certain place along the track it emerges and is identifiable as a train.

What helps make the transition from a train to a person is the thought of the Dutch theologian Edward Schillebeeckx. He observes that there is in the world an inner thrust toward rendering explicit what has hitherto remained anonymous, individualized, and internalized, namely a slowly emerging responsibility on the part of politics and secular culture for the liberation and humanization of life, the establishing of justice, the securing of economic well-being for all, and the assurance of peace.[6]

Schillebeeckx's idea relates to both people and Christ, in the thought pattern of the theological left. The reader who prefers a catchier concept than the Dutchman's rather abstract explanation can find it in a phrase employed by H.R. Niebuhr. Near the end of *Christ and Culture* he gives a name to the hidden activity of God in Christ—the Great Surd.[7] He mentions it momentarily, leaving it to the reader to make the connection. According to *The Oxford Universal Dictionary,* "surd" is a number that cannot be expressed in finite terms; in phonetics, it is a speech sound uttered without a voice or without the vibrations of the vocal chord.[8] In the context of Niebuhr's thought, therefore, surd is the activity of God motivating people today, apart from their conscious faith in him and from their understanding of Scripture.

In a biblical context, however, God is not without a voice, or vocal chords, for that matter. It is the privilege and mission of the Church to make public his activity and the Source that is behind it. Through the Church, the Living Word bears witness to the Surd. Describing this activity, labeling it, and relating it to contemporary events and persons is the work of the Word. Jesus Christ, the Word, is just as interested in human beings receiving a faith-awareness of God's presence and priorities today as he was in the first century. And when modern man can see that God's first-century visit has a twentieth-century phase, the power of the gospel is turned on. When the Word is not confined to a credal chair on the right hand of God the Father, the gospel motivates anew. A vision of God with people in the world becomes an incentive for faith and service, leading them and assuring them that they are not engaged alone in the quest for justice and peace. Realizing that God is met in other human beings—especially those in need—they are, as Roger Garaudy, a Marxist, observed, encouraged to turn toward the world, not away from it.[9]

The Church is that segment of society that names the Name. It is where the brackets are removed. To this must be added: removed *thoughtfully*. As any layman knows, the Name is quite consistently named during the week, but unthinkingly. Profanity is in vain, but not without meaning, except to those who employ it. There is significance in the fact that in English no other name than God's is used to punctuate a point or to ventilate frustration.[10] Quite literally Jesus becomes a curse. Moreover, I believe this irreverent cacophony is a kind of unintended or inverse witness to One who, though unrecognized, is nonetheless present in a person's mind. The Word wells up from those who do not know of God's activity outside the church building and, therefore, is unconsciously articulated.

This may be why many male members of the Church find participation in its life difficult. For many businessmen, truck drivers, and factory workers, it may be painful to go from the blue air of daily invective to the sacred chambers of the church. It requires a psychological split to switch abruptly between a climate where the Name is referred to thoughtlessly and one where the language is spoken as if it had legitimate meaning. This is another reason why laymen must be encouraged to express the focus of modern faith in their own words. If this must be done on Sunday morning during the worship service in order to meet people where they are, so be it. As long as the preacher is a surrogate for everyman's assimilation, the content of the Name will be isolated from the weekday world in which it so frequently receives dishonorable mention.

Ultimately, however, the witness of the Word to the Surd will gain credibility as justice and peace find a home among members of the human family. When what is proclaimed in the church actually begins to shape the lifestyle of the world, the efficacy of the Word will be much stronger. When the work of the Surd and the Word converge, the consummation will have taken place. The train will have emerged. The Christ through whom God holds all things together will have been recognized as such. When the kingdom of justice, peace, and faith has been brought to fulfillment, Jesus will have returned. If we think of the Second Coming in this way, we see that the future eschatological goal is constantly approaching humanity, or humanity it. Christ, the Word of God, is coming through each generation.[11] He is on the way even though he has been and is here with us all the time as the Great Surd.

Jurgen Moltmann, another German theologian, moves my thought in this direction when he writes, "God . . . never exhausts himself in any historic reality but comes 'to rest' only in a reality that wholly corresponds to him."[12] Until a reality is created that wholly accords with his promises, he must work for change. Moltmann sees the gospel as identical with the reconciliation of the godless and with the instituting of "believing obedience." He does not see Christianity as a religion that is one possibility among others, but as being the way to true humanity, to that which is appointed for all men (and women).[13]

I know that this viewpoint will make some people's hair stand on conservative end. There are those who see the world getting worse and worse; they will no doubt be disappointed to read of someone suggesting that it is proceeding in a more hopeful direction, because of the activity of God. Billy Graham feels that time is running out. "There's one minute left in the last quarter," he observed over national television. And although Hal Lindsay does not claim to know the day and hour, he has written a book about *The Late Great Planet Earth.*[14]

Those who draw their spiritual breath in this kind of apocalyptic atmosphere exhale the feeling that this world is a hopeless situation and, since its fate is irreversible (and irredeemable), the only sure thing is the life of the world to come. Redeeming all society is impossible. The only recourse is to save as many as are willing to accept the means of escape made possible through Jesus. Believing that the Lord of history is going to pronounce closing time on all human enterprise—and soon—there is no point in trying to improve things. With such words in print I can see Karl Marx sitting up in his grave.

It must be acknowledged, of course, that such views find their reference in Scripture as well as in present-day thought. The book of Revelation is the prime source: God waits until the Antichrist has had his day, and things reach such a level of deterioration that Christ can appear and be recognized by contrast.[15] Then he claims as his own those who have not faded into the ungodly foliage.[16] However, my view of the Second Coming takes into account the human tendency to make God in man's image (this is the opposite of God's having made himself in man's image in Jesus). Even in the Bible there is evidence of this. The "revelation" that the heavenly bodies and earth with all of its unbelieving inhabitants will be destroyed is impossible to square with the thinking of Paul that it is God's plan to reconcile all things in Christ through his cross (Col. 1:20). The fire and brimstone sound very much like what the sons of thunder wanted Jesus to call down upon the indifferent, an idea Jesus rejected, both in principle and in practice (Mark 3:17; Luke 9:54–55). Moreover, vengeance, be it in man's nature or in God's prerogative, does not harmonize with the love that surpasses fear and punishment and endures forever (John 4:18; 1 Cor. 13:7–8). It only matches the way a driver feels when he gets behind someone traveling twenty mph in a forty mph zone.

Indeed, no one waits until the end to experience judgment. Albert Camus is not the only one who knows that it takes place every day. However, he described the human experience very well when he wrote, regarding the Last Judgment, "Allow me to laugh respectfully. I shall wait for it resolutely, for I have known what is worse, the judgment of men. Men allow for no extenuating circumstances; they even ascribe criminal motive to a good intention." Then, after his reference to the "spitting cell" he concluded: "That is a human invention. They didn't need God for that little masterpiece."[17] In other words, Armageddon would be a breeze for the people of Vietnam compared to what they have been through for the past twenty years.

I recognize that my view of the return of Christ goes counter to Matthew's description of the Parousia, coming as brilliantly as the flashing of lightning from the East to the West, an interpretation supported by Daniel's prophecy of the Son of Man coming on the clouds (Matt. 24:27–30; Dan. 7:11–14). I also realize that this seems alien to the words of the "two men in white robes" who informed the disciples at the time of the Ascension that Jesus "will come in the same way as you saw him go into heaven" (Acts 1:10–11). On the other hand, the interpretation of the return that I am affirming does take into account the difference between the world view of the first century and that of the twentieth. A visible descent to earth by Christ probably would have made sense to people who believed the world was flat and who live in or near Jerusalem. But the disciples, who were told that Jesus would return in the same way he departed, are long gone, along with their world view. A spherical planet creates a different situation, one of which not even Jesus revealed an awareness. (But then, at that time, he did not need to know. He was not communicating with people whose world view had been illuminated by science.) Were Jesus visibly to descend from the skies today, were the Parousia to be via parachute, not everyone would see it, even if he advised CBS, NBC, and ABC in advance. Maybe someday, when all the Pygmies in Africa, the Aborigines in Australia, the Mongolians in China, and the Peruvians in South America have television, it will occur this way.

But it is not necessary to consider the return of Christ in external terms only. The eye of faith would take on the dimension of sight were the world to be a kingdom of justice and peace, where darkness was dispelled by the Word of light, reflected in the message of the theological left.

Finally, I also recognize that my view of the return of Christ goes counter to the futurism of Karl Marx, who asserted that with the dawn of a just society the need for religion would disappear, as a man who has been cured throws away his crutches. I agree that the need for a spiritual crutch will vanish, and, as the body of Christ becomes explicit in humanity as a whole, the Church may in some way lose itself in the world. However, should this happen, in the process the Church will find itself everywhere, for what will also disappear will be unbelief. "Atheism does not seem to be a fundamental doctrine of Marxism, except as the antithesis to a God who is pictured as the original creator and guarantor of the social and economic systems that enslave and oppress."[18] Remove the thesis and the antithesis also evaporates.

Marx was so close to biblical thought, merely substituting history for God in his earthbound view of the future. He readily admitted that what he was proposing would probably not occur in his lifetime, or in that of any of his contemporaries. Consequently, he felt the need for a concept that would last long enough to provide people with faith and vision, and that concept was history. (For him, history was economically determined.) So again he turned to Judeo-Christian belief to find for his own use an absolute goal for humankind. In other words, he deified history. He did not name the Name, but he borrowed the content, end, and process that belong to that Name. In accepting the Beyond, not as an otherworldly dimension but as one to be implemented on earth, he was responding to the Lord of history, and atheistic communists are no more than a Word away from finding this out. Those who have died have already discovered it.

Some say that Karl Marx manufactured his own brand of "opium for the people." He did not see pie in the sky, but he saw it on earth. However, it must be remembered that it was the New Testament that provided the basis for his vision. The issue does not rest with Marx, but with Jesus, who gave explicit expression to faith in a God who cannot work for less on earth than he knows to be his eternal plan for human beings. The future provides a safe hope, to be sure, for no one can dismiss what has not already occurred, but the future Jesus envisioned was based not on an ideal or on an hypothesis, but on what God had revealed and proved himself to be concerned about—here and now.

In saying that there is an absolute goal to history, I am not thinking of an eternal, preordained order to the world, one which gradually unfolds one step at a time. The goal exists in the mind of God, and this makes it absolute, but in working for its fulfillment on earth, history moves forward from event to event. The movement of Word and Surd toward convergence is a jagged course, and reverse motion can occur at times. Indeed, when the social and political overtones of the kingdom are suppressed in favor of the religious experience of the individual, the dynamics of the arriving kingdom are diverted from their aim of transforming the world. However, God does not give up, but relentlessly pursues his goal. We are living in a time when the motion appears to be forward.

Let the bells be silenced
Let the gifts be stillborn
Let cheer be muted
Let music be soundless

Violence stalks the land:
Soaring above the cry of the dying
Rising above the whimper of the starving
Floating above the flying machines of death

Listen to the long stillness:
New life is stirring
New dreams are on the wing

New hopes are being readied:
Mankind is fashioning a new heart
Mankind is forging a new mind
God is at work.

Howard Thurman, 1968

ISSUES FOR DISCUSSION

1. To many the kingdom of God is a heavenly arrangement designed to bypass earth.

2. God's integrity demands that, having promised the kingdom, he must seek to bring it about here and now as well as hereafter.

3. Building the earthly city has no connection with the city of God.

4. In America (and ultimately the world) there is no liberty and justice for one until there is the same for all.

5. Even in God's earthly kingdom there will be human work, sweat, and death.

6. The work of the Word and the Surd are complementary.

7. Stress on eternal salvation emerged in response to a doomsday view of the future.

8. The motifs of damnation and redemption in Scripture are compatible.

9. The return of Christ can be thought of in other terms than that of a visible descent from the sky.

NOTES

1. See Edouard Beauduin, "Faith, the Principal Requirement of Christian Unity," *Lumen Vitae* 23 (1968), p. 25.

2. Concerning injustice, one young person said, "All you have to do is open your eyes, man. If it don't make you sick, ain't nothin' no one can do for you."

3. Burrhus Frederic Skinner, *Walden II* (New York: Macmillan, 1948). Skinner's example of model functions in a rather isolated relationship to the rest of society, an oasis in a desert.

4. "The Unity of the Church and the Unity of Mankind," *Ecumenical Press Service,* November 9, 1969, p. 16.

5. See Carl E. Braaten, *Christ and Counter-Christ* (Philadelphia: Fortress Press, 1972) and Peter Hodgson, *Jesus–Word and Presence* (Philadelphia: Fortress Press, 1971), p. 88.

6. "The Church and Mankind," Concilium, vol. I, p. 85.

7. H. R. Niebuhr, *Christ and Culture* (New York: Harper, 1951), p. 255.

8. What Marx as a youth referred to as the "innermost voice" relates to this.

9. Garaudy sees the Incarnation as meaning that Christ, the Living God, is standing before us. "Communist and Christian in Dialogue," *New Theology,* no. 5 (New York: Macmillan, 1968), p. 219.

10. See my article, "Jesus Christ—the Household Word," *Lutheran Forum,* November 1973, pp. 18, 20.

11. There is an eschatological significance to his love for children.

12. Jurgen Moltmann, *Theology of Hope* (New York: Harper, 1965), p. 106.

13. *Ibid.,* p. 286. This is one way to understand Jesus' words, "I am the way. . . . No one comes to the Father but by me" (John 14:6).

14. Hal Lindsey, *The Late Great Planet Earth* (Grand Rapids: Zondervan, 1970).

15. Ezek. 38:14–23; Rev. 20:14–15. People of every age feel theirs is the worst so far, and such sensitivity belongs to the process of truth and purgation.

16. Eustace Percy writes that the narrowing of human destiny to a bare choice between heaven and hell has been the universal assumption of the Church for at least a thousand years, ever since the early Christian's hope of Christ's second coming was blotted out by the terrors of the Day of Judgment (*John Knox* [Richmond: John Knox Press, 1965], p. 108).

17. Albert Camus, *The Fall* (New York: Knopf, 1961), p. 110. Prisoners were placed in a narrow cell where they could not protect their faces, and then people passed by and spat on them.

18. Carl E. Braaten, *Christ and Counter-Christ,* p. 35.